P9-AOF-185

The
Artful Journal

A Spiritual Quest

The
Artful Journal

A Spiritual Quest

MAUREEN CAREY ✑ RAYMOND FOX ✑ JACQUELINE PENNEY

WATSON-GUPTILL PUBLICATIONS ✑ NEW YORK

First published in 2002 by
Watson-Guptill Publications
a division of VNU Business Media, Inc.
770 Broadway, New York, NY 10003
www.watsonguptill.com

Senior Editor: Candace Raney
Editor: Gabrielle Pecarsky
Designer: Areta Buk
Production Manager: Hector Campbell

Library of Congress Cataloging-in-Publication Data

Carey, Maureen.
    The artful journal : a spiritual quest / Maureen Carey, Raymond Fox,
and Jacqueline Penney.
    p. cm.
Includes bibliographical references and index.
ISBN 0-8230-0320-5
    1. Spirituality.   2. Creative ability—Religious aspects.   3. Art and
religion.   I. Fox, Raymond.   II. Penney, Jacqueline.   III. Title.
BL624 .C3465 2001
291.4'46—dc21

                              2001005269

Printed in Hong Kong

First printing, 2002

1 2 3 4 5 6 7 8 9 / 08 07 06 05 04 03 02

TO ALL SEEKERS . . .

THOSE DARING TO TAKE THE JOURNEY

TO THE VERY CORE OF SELF AND SPIRIT.

Contents

Introduction

THERE ARE MANY WAYS to understand, experience, and express spirituality. In American culture there seems to be a renewed hunger for and focus on the transcendent. Spirituality, as distinct from religion, orients the human person toward ultimate values and priorities. A slow but steady shift that emphasizes the importance of spiritual issues is occurring in such fields as psychology, social work, and medicine. These professions are researching how the spirit, indeed one's spirituality, makes humans whole. There is evidence that mental and physical health and well-being are positively correlated in people who have some kind of spiritual practice.

The Artful Journal: A Spiritual Quest provides a way for processing the spiritual dimensions of your life by incorporating the creative process into the daily practice of meditation. The motivation of the authors to write this book arises from this growing desire among seekers to find ways to cultivate a spiritual life. A substantial and growing number of mental health professionals describe spirituality as the single most important source of strength and direction in life.

The authors of *The Artful Journal: A Spiritual Quest* have, for a number of years, offered workshops devoted to the power of journal keeping during many art and spiritual retreats. This idea originated when Maureen went on an eight-day silent retreat, where she incorporated pen and ink "doodles" on a page alongside written reflections that elaborated the meaning of the drawing in relationship to the experience of prayer just completed. It was a way to "give voice" to the experience of prayer, an act that is often hard to articulate. Quite by chance, Maureen was given a blank journal containing very heavy, water-absorbent paper. It occurred to her that she could easily splash color onto the page, draw with pen and ink, and write reflections. Out of this experience, our workshop was born.

It is actually at the insistence of many of our workshop participants that this book has come to be

The figure, prostrate in supplication, almost blending with the earth, takes nourishment from the earth and transforms it into energy.

written. It encompasses a great deal of the content we offer at these retreats, but, more importantly, it includes, as illustrative examples, the poignant results from participants who risked blending color with words in their journals both during their stay at the retreat and beyond. *The Artful Journal: A Spiritual Quest* also includes an array of works by the authors, who themselves continually risked experimenting with new artistic directions and spiritual exercises, even as they conducted the workshops.

This book also comes out of the authors' personal and professional experiences supporting the idea that spirituality and creativity may be inherently linked. The spiritual dimension influences and shapes the creative; the creative resides most fully within the spiritual realm. Has there not always been an intuitive link between the artistic and the creative; between the artist and the mystic?

Dropping color, allowing the pigments to blend, and using a wet brush to pull the colors upward, soften the predominantly horizontal shape below. The mindless pen-and-ink doodle enhances the painting and makes it more meaningful.

We suggest that daily meditation practice combined with the integration of watercolor and words promotes this work of the spirit. This method, really a "non" method, can be captured by the seasoned artist and the beginner alike. We emphasize a way to attend to one's spiritual development as the starting point rather than to describe a precise step-by-step method of art instruction. We offer suggestions and directions. We provide a way of harnessing the rich and fertile movements of the soul by tapping your creative right brain. We recommend dropping watercolor onto journal pages to enhance your inner reflections from prayer. We focus on expressing prayer with color, doodles, and words.

Gaining self-knowledge and insight comes from a disciplined, daily look at the reality of your life and your relationship with yourself, with others, and, perhaps, with God. From the ordinary, seemingly unimportant aspects of your life, growth and movement blossom.

The Artful Journal: A Spiritual Quest emphasizes regular journal use to process your "inner" life, springing you forward to a fuller, richer, and more expressive "outer" life. When you face the ordinary, daily events in your life with persistence and attention, and place them within the context of the sacred, growth and maturation are natural by-products.

We sincerely hope that *The Artful Journal: A Spiritual Quest* encourages you to start keeping a journal or renews your commitment to maintaining your present one. We also expect that in delving into the process of combining color and words you will find the practice of journal keeping greatly enhanced. More importantly, we trust that through this process you contact new, more meaningful, and more fulfilling places both in your heart and in your soul.

Chapter 1

Launching Your Spiritual and Creative Journal

We sit silently and watch the world around us.
This has taken us a lifetime to learn . . . for
silence is pure. Silence is holy. It draws people
together . . . this is the great paradox.

NICHOLAS SPARKS

A<small>S WE BEGIN</small> together an exploration of journal keeping that uses watercolor, images, and words, let's first look at some of the key reasons why this type of journal is worthwhile and provides insight and opportunity for growth. The following Ten Principles of Journaling set the stage for embarking on this journey into self-discovery and growth.

Ten Principles of Journaling

1. JOURNALING IS A JOURNEY OF THE SPIRIT

Some of you are inclined to be painters, others writers, and still others photographers. Some of you use pigments, some words, some pen, pencil, or pastels, yet others cameras. Whatever your inclination, whatever your medium, you are, all of you, artists. As artists you are, all of you, seekers. You all journey to find spirituality, creativity, peace, comfort, wholeness, transcendence.

2. JOURNALING HELPS NAVIGATE YOUR VOYAGE OF DISCOVERY

Since the artist has an intuitively spiritual nature that requires nurturing for artistic development, the journal that incorporates painting, drawing, and reflections in words can produce personal growth and enhance creativity.

Some of you are new to journaling. Some of you have been at it for years. Whatever your previous experience with journaling, all of you know down deep in your hearts that paintings and drawings, images, prose and poetry are extremely powerful. They simultaneously express and expose who you are.

For those of you who already journal, who are, as it were, in the fall of your journey, this book is an invitation to turn yet another leaf. It introduces alternative and creative ways to uncover yourself. For those of you new to journaling, in the spring of your journey, this book is an invitation to find a deeper self through journaling.

The warm fluid colors and the ribbons of connected dots enhance the flame-like curls that emanate from the figure in a pose of deep reverence.

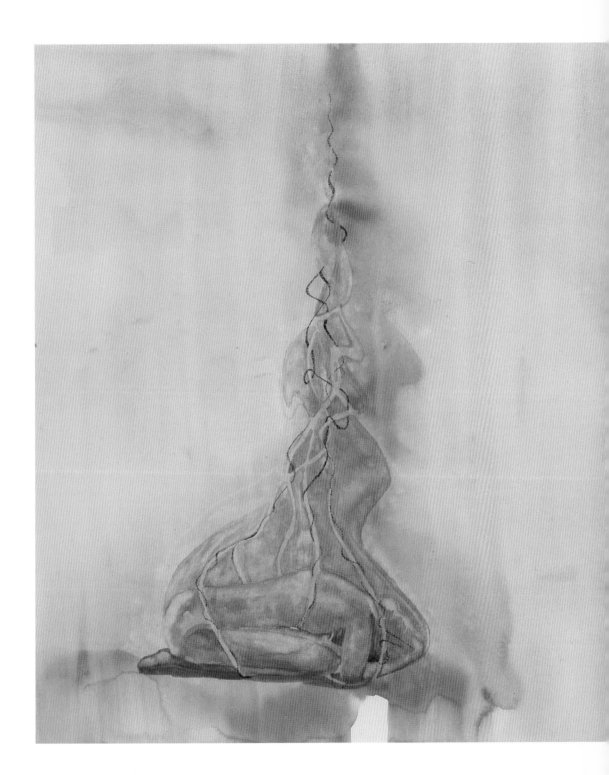

3. Journaling Takes Courage to Go Within

To journal—through painting, images, words, and perhaps, down the road, a blend of all three—requires a decision, a decision that takes courage. Courage to start a journal. Courage to undertake committing your stirrings—ideas, thoughts, feelings, prayers—to paper. Courage, because, in so doing, you face your "self."

Many famous people have journaled. And their journals chronicled their lives, related or relived their experiences, or simply focused their attention. All were courageous, yet courageous for different reasons. You'll recognize some of their names: Eugène Delacroix—of the great artists, clearly the greatest writer—Anne Frank, Etty Hillston, Samuel Pepys, Anais Nin. You'll be in good company as you journal.

The journals of the famous diarists do not focus simply on problems, concerns, or regrets: on negatives. Although much popular writing about journals touts their usefulness in overcoming stressful events, discontent, distress, and worry, the journal can also be a source of joy, creativity, and serenity. Oprah Winfrey, over and over again, has lauded the benefit of the "gratitude" journal. It can help you to discover your own voice, perhaps literally compose your own "life script."

4. Journaling Opens a Path to Serendipity

A journal awakens the heart, mind, and spirit to new experiences and new horizons. Even if you are impelled to journal, it doesn't just automatically happen. To proceed, you need to put brush to paper, pen to pad. In choosing to proceed, you open yourself to serendipity. But you also face the prospect of unearthing what lies buried within you, remains dormant, and is hidden from yourself.

This complicated, well-defined pen-and-ink image attached to a distant, linear landscape uniquely illustrates the essence of self.

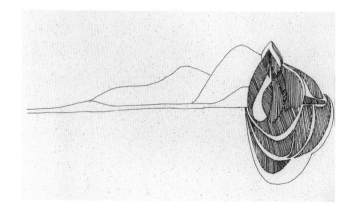

5. Journaling Takes Time

Keeping a journal is not intended to save time, but rather to savor time. While the process consumes time and is difficult—even haltingly and frightfully painful at junctures along the way, because either nothing or too much comes to the surface—when you step forward and press onward, the journal can be exhilarating, freeing, and illuminating.

Take time to dwell with your "self." Contact your "spirit." And even though it takes time, you are worth the time. Devote time to discovering your inner life. While some may consider it lavish, excessive, indeed selfish of you to do so, that is not the case. Journaling helps you to find your "selfness." After all, Socrates recommended, "Know thyself." And Shakespeare cautioned, "To thine own self be true . . ."

6. Journaling Invites Self-Knowledge

Journaling in no way makes you "selfish." Being selfish conveys self-indulgence, self-involvement, self-reference. It involves insensitivity, or even neglect or abuse, of other people, interest only in the promotion of self. Often, the opposite of what is called selfish is referred to as being "self-less." Being self-less, however, entails a loss of individuality, a suppression of the uniquely personal. Oftentimes it renders one invisible and remote to others. Having "selfness" conveys precisely what Socrates and Shakespeare mean by being true to your "self." It means acknowledging, accepting, and celebrating your distinct essence, spirit, and soul. It is being faithful to the Biblical injunction to love yourself.

At a retreat, Raymond, reflecting on this concept, entered the following:

> The words, "journal" and "journey," interestingly, have the same Latin root: "daily." Journaling, then, promotes a regular, although sometimes unscheduled, journey inward to your inner life. It allows you to inhabit your subjective space, and to do so safely. It is a journey of the spirit. The Little Prince said, "It is only with the heart that one can see rightly." The journal heals and empowers you. It heartens self-discovery and "inner-centeredness." It unleashes inner strengths.

Because most of your advances toward enlightenment and fulfillment are gradual and usually imperceptible, an added bonus of the journal is that it provides a tangible record marking your growth, movement, and progress.

We all understand the meaning of the words "selfish" and "selfless." Raymond coined the word "selfness," which to him means acknowledging, accepting, and celebrating your distinct essence, spirit, and soul. This realistic rendering at a retreat inspired the written reflection, which continued, as if it were part of the scene, artistically adding to the composition.

GOD, YOU DRAW ME OUT OF THE WATER
   THE WINDING MOVEMENT CURVING
INTO NEW OPENINGS & NEW VIEWS OF
THIS LANDSCAPE LIFE OF MINE.
   AND, TODAY YOU DRAW ME, PULL ME,
      LIFT ME OUT OF THE WATERS
   & YOU TAKE ME HOME.
      WHAT IS THIS LIFTING-OUT & WHY?
IT IS THE GIFT OF SELF-NESS... OF SELF-POSSESSION

TUESDAY
7/13

7. JOURNALING FURTHERS SYNCHRONICITY

Unhurried and relaxed concentration in the silence and solitude of your own special space brings with it a sense of tranquility, as is evident in this journal entry:

> *Inward mindfulness and inward attention open the way for synchronicity. Synchronicity is an unexpected and delightful happening that occurs unbidden. It is interesting to note that in watercolor, for example, "accidents" or blossoms are frequently even more beautiful and captivating than any deliberate or conscious act of painting. Likewise, in writing, word "slips" often more accurately capture the true significance of what you mean than what you intended to write. Both, possibly, are serendipitous messages from your unconscious.*

The journal sets the course for providence.

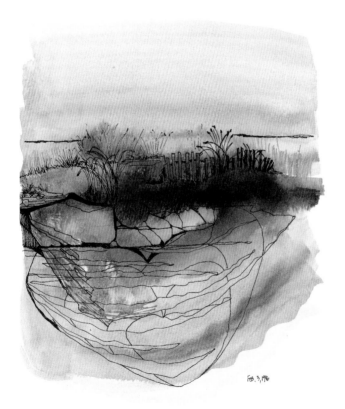

Feb. 3, 1996

LEFT: *Silence and solitude in your own special space can bring with it a sense of tranquility. The horizontal theme and soft curvilinear shapes on—or even possibly beneath—the water speak of deep subconscious thought.*

OPPOSITE: *Synchronicity is an unexpected and delightful happening that occurs unbidden. Watercolor "accidents" known as blossoms can be even more beautiful and captivating than any planned, deliberate, or conscious act of painting. The accidents or blossoms within the taped-off area become the ground for the simple, linear landscape.*

MAY, 1999

SHELTER THE WORD,
 MOVING INTO THE UNKNOWN
ITINERANT PREACHER OF A
 NEWS THAT IS SO
 POWERFUL &
 SO REAL – IT CAN
CHANGE LIVES & ALTER COURSES.
GOD OF THIS JOURNEY, I AM CALLED TO
LET GO OF MY CLAIM ON MY LIFE. IT IS
NO LONGER OF MY MAKING. LEAD ME
INTO YOUR FUTURE. I AM FEARFUL. I AM
RESISTANT. I LACK COURAGE & I AM TRULY
NOT... ENOUGH. BE THE FEARLESSNESS & THE COURAGE & THE
STRENGTH OF CONVICTION THAT I NEED. LET ME KNOW MY WAY! HOME

8. JOURNALING HAS NO LIMITS

While there are formal rules and principles for painting and for writing, these rarely apply when journaling. Formulas merely interfere with the process as it unfolds naturally. There are neither right nor wrong ways of doing it. Likewise, there are no limits, no restraints. You can design—and redesign—your journal process to work for you. Whatever you wish it to reflect, however you want it to flow, whichever tools you select, the journal is uniquely yours.

Journaling, in other words, is a dynamic, not a static endeavor. It is continuous, and in flux. It grows through you. You grow through it.

Exercise: Life Questions

The hardest part of talking about the journal is its transcendent and transformative value. It enables you to reach into but, at the same time, seemingly contradictorily, extend your self to ever higher levels of consciousness. Words that describe the process—sacred, awesome, wondrous—do not quite depict the profound spiritual and inspirational character of the journal. In quiet wonder, the journal inspires without reason, touches your innermost spirit. It unfolds new "lifescapes."

For this exercise, the following questions are posed. They provide a guidepost, a map for you to consider in beginning your journal. As you notice throughout this book, every attempt is made to remain true to its theme—undertaking an inward journey. The following questions are merely suggestive. You can adopt them or adapt them, making them work for you in initiating your trip toward your spiritual center. Take your time. Try to proceed without conscious direction, censoring, or editing.

Who was I?
Who am I?
Who will I be?
How will I know when I've arrived?
What will I find inside?

No rules apply. Just begin to write your responses and reflections. Let them flow.

9. Journaling Is a Private Matter of the Heart

Some of you may feel shy, reluctant, and possibly hesitant about allowing other people to have access to your private world. Remember this: even though you may decide to exhibit a painting in a journal, or publish an excerpt or whole journal entry in words, such public sharing will neither fully represent you nor expose you. That is, the private process you undergo to produce it is yours alone.

10. Journaling Paves the Way Toward a Sacred Space

Above all else, your journal provides a safe harbor from which to launch a journey of self-discovery and illumination. All of us, at one time or another, yearn for a "safehouse," a "healing place," or a "sacred space," as Joseph Campbell calls it: a refuge that allows us to get away from the din of the world, a place where literally, figuratively, and spiritually we can re-create ourselves. Your journal can be that place.

As a sacred space, it frees and extends paths for artistic expression as it opens and expands the possibilities for mindful awareness, creative experimentation, and spiritual revelation.

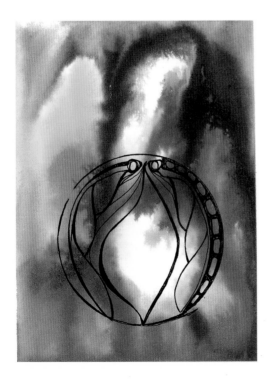

Stephen Batchelor states in his book Buddhism Without Beliefs: *"This is emptiness: not a cosmic vacuum but the 'womb of awakening,' it is the clearing in the still center of becoming, the track on which the centered person moves." Maureen created two forms within a circle that seem to resemble pubescent butterflies; the small opening within the circle suggests the "womb of awakening."*

CHAPTER 2

Meditation
for Its Own Sake

Love winter, when the plant says nothing.

THOMAS MERTON

MEDITATION PRACTICE and prayer are two
terms that are used, sometimes interchangeably, to describe the practice of
"turning within." These activities have much in common, both providing a way
for "the seeker" to get more deeply in touch with his or her spiritual self. Both
require that you center yourself, employ periods of silence, and use proper body
positions in order to gain maximum benefit from the practice. Although various
traditions define prayer and meditation differently, the term "meditation" will be
used in this book to describe all of the various types of praying or meditating.

Meditation is frequently misunderstood as only the practice of sitting or
kneeling in a set position over a period of time in total silence. This certainly
describes a common form of meditation, yet any of the many practices that still
the body and the mind into silence and communion can be considered meditation.

Some of these methods will be described in this chapter, and you may also
want to read more about meditation in some of the books listed in the Further
Reading section at the back of this book. However, it is important to emphasize
that the entire process described in this book—of sitting in silence, of dropping
color, of doodling and writing reflections, poetry, or thoughts—can be, in its
entirety, considered meditation.

This chapter encourages you and explains to you how to include a regular
period of meditation practice within your day, in tandem with journal keeping.
It is less important which particular meditation technique you employ than that
you are faithful to it. Indeed, what is essential is simply that you begin the daily,
regular practice of being still, using a journal that employs watercolor, doodles,
and reflections.

While the combination of meditation and a multimedia journal method has
not received widespread attention among practitioners in various schools of
meditation, the concept of "automatic drawing," in which the artist begins to draw
whatever comes to mind, has long been seen as a part
of mindfulness practice—a form of meditation used by
some Buddhists.

*"Love winter, when the
plant says nothing," a quote
by Thomas Merton, was
the muse for this journal
painting.*

In *The Complete Idiot's Guide to Meditation*, a section
is devoted to this concept of art as meditation. We
suggest that when you are engaged in this process of
automatic drawing, or what we describe in this book as

LOVE WINTER,
WHEN THE PLANT SAYS NOTHING.
MERTON

NOV. 18, 1995

27

"painting meditation" and "doodling meditation," you can "become one with the process. You are meditating—and creating, too!" This combined meditation process teaches you how to see the extraordinary in the ordinary, making everything look different and more beautiful.

GOD, SOURCE of ALL THAT EXISTS,
YOU BRING US TO
BIRTH
AND TO
REBIRTH IN YOUR SON.
8.14.97

Some Fundamental Premises to Meditation Practice

There are many types of meditation practice. In the Christian tradition there is contemplative prayer, centering prayer, and prayer that uses Scripture, song, and ritual. In the Eastern tradition there is a practice known as mindfulness meditation (the classic Zen Buddhist meditation) and meditation practices incorporating walking, yoga, and t'ai chi. And, of course, as just mentioned, there is also art as meditation. All of these ways of praying and meditating are available to you. Various traditions have special methods to promote growth in prayer/practice. For example, Thich Nhat Hanh, a Buddhist monk, has written extensively on the practice of mindfulness, considered a conscious attunement to all that is around and within, an awareness of each moment as it occurs and a purposeful attention. Yoga and t'ai chi are gaining in popularity, and courses on how to advance in these spiritual practices are now found in adult-education courses and at many local retreat centers. Use whatever practice is most comfortable to discover your own perspective, your own way.

WHEN TO MEDITATE

Find a regular time of the day to meditate. Choose a time when you are least likely to be disturbed by noise, phone calls, and other distractions. You may find it difficult to set a regular pattern if you perceive meditation as a chore or "one more thing to do." However, keep in mind that discipline is the first step to freedom. Finding the time to waste time is a paradox.

Understanding the importance of meditation may be the first breakthrough you have as you incorporate a regular meditation practice into your busy, over-scheduled life.

For how long should you do a "silent meditation" each day? When first beginning, be realistic: sitting within the silence for five minutes may initially feel more like fifty. It may be helpful to set up a daily schedule of meditation, improving your practice time each week. For example, in week two increase the meditation time by five minutes and keep that pattern for several weeks. As you become more and more comfortable in the silence, you can increase the time in five-minute increments. To indicate the end of a session, many people use a timer to avoid the disruption of having to frequently look at a clock.

Single-pointed energy is a visual metaphor for the way that meditation impels us to give birth to our true self.

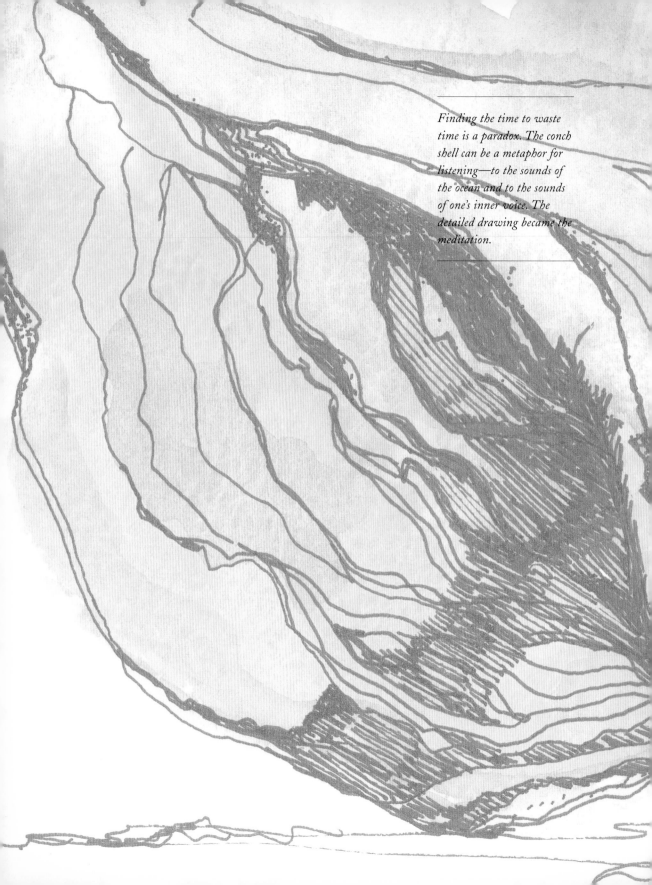

Finding the time to waste time is a paradox. The conch shell can be a metaphor for listening—to the sounds of the ocean and to the sounds of one's inner voice. The detailed drawing became the meditation.

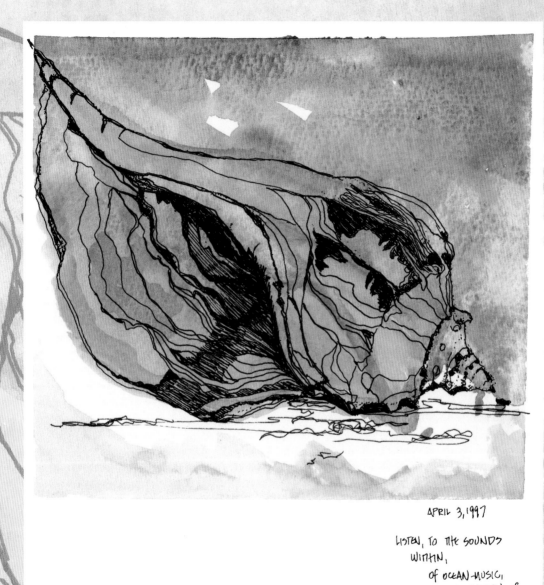

APRIL 3, 1997

LISTEN, TO THE SOUNDS
WITHIN,
OF OCEAN MUSIC,
THE MYSTERY OF
PRESENCE WITHIN.

MEDITATION POSTURE AND ENVIRONMENT

Most forms of meditation require some type of sitting position. Comfort, in combination with good posture, is the key to most. A slumped back will constrict your breathing and also lull you to sleep. It is important to keep the energy flow steady and high, and an appropriate meditation posture will do just that.

Finding a location that is conducive to meditation is very important. Select a room that is quiet and not likely to be used by others. Burning incense or lighting a candle may help to "center" you. You might consider listening to some music at the beginning of your meditation period. In this manner, music can be a centering technique, providing an avenue into a deeper silence. However, playing music during the entire session could prove to be a distraction. Through experimenting with these variables, you will find the particular method that works best for you.

Much has been written about what to focus on: your breath; the sounds within your environment; an object, such as a lit candle; the use of a mantra—the repeating of a word or phrase. Many books provide in-depth discussions of these various techniques. (You will find several listed in the Further Reading section of this book.) Whenever the mind wanders, gently bring it back to the focal point of the meditation.

Meditation and Prayer—A Waste of Time?

At the beginning, meditation may feel like a waste of time, for "nothing is happening." Precisely! Bo Lozoff, a practitioner of meditation who has written about the subject, says that meditation is the opposite of the expression, "Don't just sit there—do something." Meditation or prayer insists, "Don't just do something— sit there." Yes, waste time—with God, with self-discovery, with finding your true self. There is no greater gift you can give to others each day than *you*, the true self. Anthony Padavano, in describing Trappist monk Thomas Merton's notion of the true self, says: "The most fundamental of all our vocations is the calling . . . to become ourselves. All else we do can be done as well or better by others except this one and absolutely unique responsibility . . . to be who we must be."

A quote by Anthony Padavano is enclosed within a sphere that simply encapsulates rich meaning. "All our journeys begin as human journeys. It is only later that they become consciously spiritual. It is a central truth that God became part of the human family. That is always where God is to be found."

ALL OUR JOURNEYS BEGIN AS HUMAN JOURNEYS. IT IS ONLY
LATER THAT THEY BECOME CONSCIOUSLY SPIRITUAL.
IT IS A CENTRAL TRUTH THAT GOD BECAME PART OF THE
HUMAN FAMILY. THAT IS ALWAYS WHERE GOD IS TO BE
FOUND.   PADAVANO.

SUNDAY 3/21/99

THANKSGIVING MORNING, 1995

TO BE THANKFUL, IS FOR ME THIS YEAR,
NEW ... IT IS THE SPACE WITHIN
THAT IS FREE & OPEN & IS NOT
CLAIMED BY ANY OTHER PART OF
WHAT I NEED TO GET THRU A DAY...
AND THAT PLACE IS IN THE CENTER,
EXPANSIVE & FLOWERING ALL THE
TIME... AND TO BE THANKFUL IS
THAT AWARENESS OF THE BEAUTY
FLOWERING — FIRST WITHIN & BEING
ABLE TO ALLOW IT TO GROW & THAT
GROWTH IS PROVIDING OPPORTUNITY
TO MEET & RE-MEET ALL THE
PEOPLE I LOVE & CARE FOR —
LIFE IN ITS FULLNESS,

Benefits

This practice of "doing nothing" is the basis for human transformation, not only within the self, but also within society. This paradox, found within all the spiritual traditions, suggests that it is within apparent emptiness that you find true meaning; it is within the process of letting go that you discover the essence of life. Meditation and prayer provide the proper context for viewing yourself honestly and fully. Your self-serving ego is slowly uprooted and your true nature emerges.

Willigis Jäger, a Benedictine monk who has written extensively on contemplative prayer, describes this altered view of life as "a transformation of consciousness and a view of the world that transcends the narrow circle of ego-consciousness. In turn, the transformed personality gives rise to different purposes, value judgments, and modes of behavior."

The process of transformation leads to a more forgiving, a more compassionate, and a more loving outlook. Slowly you come to yearn for a simpler way of life. There is a perspective that is attractive to others for it is rooted in truth: the truth of who you are and the truth about the meaning of life.

GROWTH IN SELF-KNOWLEDGE

To take time, to be still within the silence, to do "no-thing" is exactly what is needed to move to this deep well of self-reflection. The practice of meditation involves your putting aside the deliberate trains of thought or self-examination. Stand back from yourself and proceed to observe implicit thoughts, desires, and fears that previously may have gone unrecognized.

Combining prayer or meditation with drawing, painting, and writing in a journal unites the creative and contemplative. The key is to select a practice combination that works best for you. Automatic drawing, dropping color, abstract sketching, focused drawing on an object in the room, blind contour drawing—all are ways to extend the period of meditation.

This journal entry from Thanksgiving morning conveys the starkness of the barren tree and winter sky above the ground, as life "blossoms" and "flowers" within. The pattern of lines in the negative area around the flowers further extended the period of meditation.

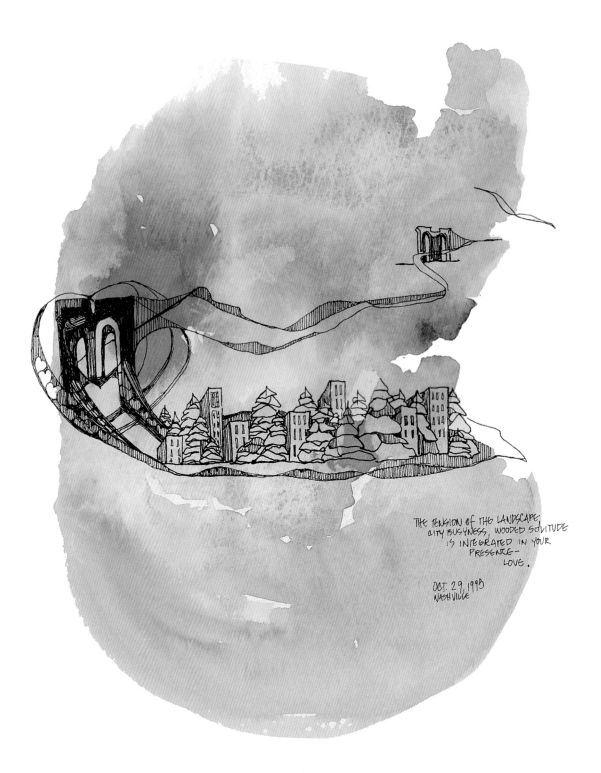

THE TENSION OF THE LANDSCAPE:
CITY BUSYNESS, WOODED SOLITUDE
IS INTEGRATED IN YOUR
PRESENCE—
LOVE.

OCT. 29, 1993
NASHVILLE

36

To wake up to yourself—to your true nature—is the journey you are called to embark on in this life. As you become more aware, the process of prayer or meditation becomes an indispensable part of your day. It no longer is the chore or the next thing on the list of things to do each day. It becomes the focal point, and daily life is slowly changed.

Exercise: Being Meditative

Find a quiet, unadorned space where you can sit comfortably for at least five minutes. If it is helpful, set a timer to alert you when this time has elapsed. In this way, you can fully concentrate on the meditative process. Assume an erect posture in whichever position facilitates in you a sense of attentiveness. Such a stance enhances the flow of breathing and helps to center you. Allow yourself to become conscious of your breathing, being mindful of your inhalations and exhalations. Focus your attention on the rhythm of your breath taking. Be still, and welcome the solitude and quiet. If your thoughts wander, gently allow yourself to re-focus on your breath.

After this period, take time for reflection and note your experience in your mind and then on paper.

Practice this process over time, gradually increasing the time spent in contemplative meditation.

This journal painting seems to reiterate the need for peacefulness, even when circumstances in our daily lives are stressful and difficult.

CHAPTER 3

Charting Your Course with Words

Our subjectivity is our true home, our natural state, and our necessary place of refuge and renewal. It is the font of creativity, the stage for imagination, the drafting table for planning, and the ultimate heart of our fears and hopes, our sorrows and satisfactions.

JAMES BUGENTAL

Writing in your journal promotes honest self-disclosure and intensive self-discovery and helps you to capture ideas, feelings, and behavior in unique ways. It is a powerful tool for developing heightened self-awareness. It adds coherence to memories, fantasies, thoughts, and intuitions. Its impact is great, invariably leading to deeper understanding. Words are powerful. They can clarify your perceptions, break impasses, and expand your horizons. Writing enables you to recognize your strengths, talents, gifts, and attributes.

Journaling can be particularly helpful if you find it difficult to acknowledge your own strengths, trust your own capacities, or appreciate your own skills. Just "doing" the journal builds your ego, offers a fresh start, opens up novel possibilities, and frees your imagination for creativity. In other words, it helps you find your spiritual core.

Words, especially when color is added to them—or they are added to color (as described in detail in Chapter 5)—paint a picture of your emotional, psychological, and spiritual landscape.

Your journal's tableau can vary in its forms—concise outline, lengthy letter, essay, scattered phrases or words, structured exercises, open-ended free association. It can take different forms at different times in your life, even at different times of the day. It is adaptable. Whatever form your journal takes, it helps you to access memories, dreams, goals, joys, hurts, and triumphs, and to come to understand them, and yourself, better. The very way you express yourself offers a transparency of your life projected onto the journal page.

Write your journal in a non-constrained and creative way. Be spontaneous. Refer to it often. Use it flexibly. For example, you might read it at the beginning of your day, meditate on it, or concentrate on it exclusively. You might select portions of it to discuss with someone else or put it aside to peruse at another time. However you use it depends upon the circumstances of your life at any one moment in time.

If you choose not to use the journal each day, don't feel compelled to force it. Write and paint without concern for how others might perceive you and don't judge it yourself. Keep writing and painting and accept the words and images that come to you.

The horizontal motif of seemingly still water is repeated in linear form with words about forgiveness. The dark, rocky bottom conveys deep feelings; the three ink drawings work almost like exclamation points to emphasize the words.

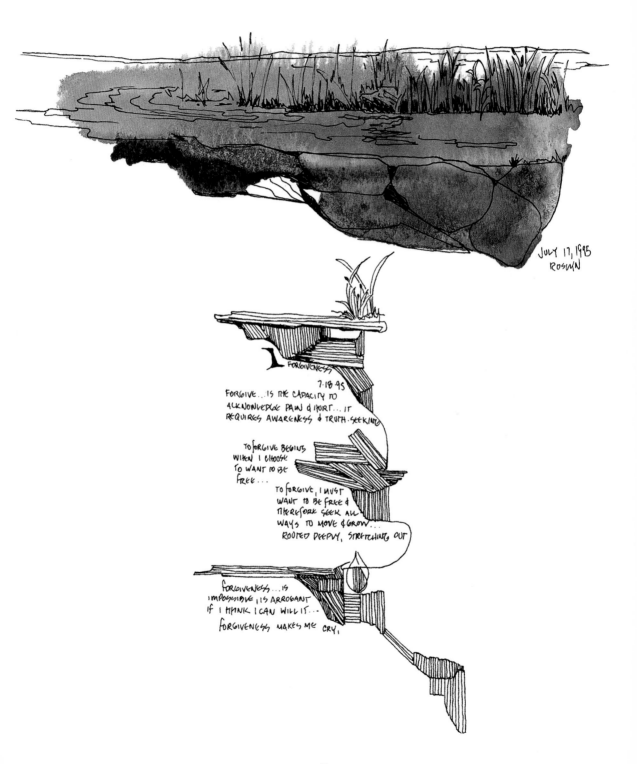

JULY 17, 1995
ROSLYN

FORGIVENESS
7·18·95

FORGIVE... IS THE CAPACITY TO
ACKNOWLEDGE PAIN & HURT... IT
REQUIRES AWARENESS & TRUTH·SEEKING

TO FORGIVE BEGINS
WHEN I CHOOSE
TO WANT TO BE
FREE...

TO FORGIVE, I MUST
WANT TO BE FREE &
THEREFORE SEEK ALL
WAYS TO MOVE & GROW...
ROOTED DEEPLY, STRETCHING OUT

FORGIVENESS... IS
IMPOSSIBLE, ITS ARROGANT
IF I THINK I CAN WILL IT...
FORGIVENESS MAKES ME CRY.

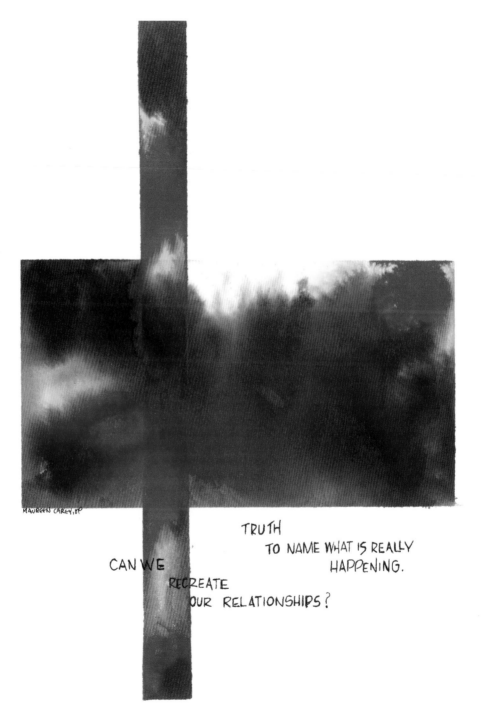

MAUREEN CAREY, OP

TRUTH
TO NAME WHAT IS REALLY
HAPPENING.

CAN WE
RECREATE
OUR RELATIONSHIPS?

SATURDAY · STIRRING THE HEART   8·21·99

Customizing Your Journal: Creative Journal Methods

There are many creative ways to customize your journal, ways for making it uniquely yours. A variety of methods, described below, is offered for you to adopt or to adapt. More importantly, considering these may actually spark inventing your own original and innovative means for capturing ideas, thoughts, feelings, dreams, and discoveries.

"Scrapbooking"

For Peter, a participant on one of our retreats who had been a foster care child nearly all his life, the journal, or "scrapbook," as he called it, was his declaration of identity. Shuttled between eight foster homes within twelve years, he had always felt lost and alone, "a stranger in a strange land." Into his scrapbook he organized photographs and mementos from an array of homes, which he had, over many years, accumulated and secreted in different places. Slowly yet methodically he compiled the scrapbook, gathering all the disparate pieces of his life into one unified whole. Piecing together the fragments of his life, he clarified his memory of events and of himself. As he grew older, his "scrapbook" became a sourcebook of significant life milestones. Snapshots, baseball cards, ticket stubs, library cards, official documents, and other keepsakes, all with significant memory traces, were glued in. They helped him find and define himself: Peter repaired a fractured sense of self and established a firm identity through his journal.

"Diajournaling"

Susan, an aspiring actress, suffered from severe anxiety, stage fright, and a profound sense of inadequacy. In her journal, she unleashed her thoughts and images in the form of dramatic dialogue. Her "diajournal," as she called it, resembled a play script, allowing her to express poignantly the two-sided conflicts she felt within herself. Susan discovered that the diajournal represented polarities of her inner self. Articulating her dichotomous modes of thinking, feeling, and behaving, Susan's journal served as a source of better understanding her own personal long-standing problems with acting.

The bold letters, asking a provocative question about relationships, balance the vivid colors dropped into a cruciform shape.

THIS MORNING... TIME OF SETTLING IN & SETTLING DOWN —
& EASING INTO THIS MOST NEEDED, ABSOLUTE REFLECTION TIME

PREACHING ABOUT BECOMING FREE... THE EXODUS STORY
& THE MOVEMENT OUT... "PULLING OUT" THAT WHICH KEEPS ME
HERE. THE IDEA OF BEING INCARNATIONALIZED... BECOMING
ONE WITH WHERE YOU ARE... AS JESUS BECAME TOTALLY LIKE US
& SO, HOW HARD IT IS TO BE... IN A FOREIGN LAND
& BECOME COMFORTABLE...

CAN I BE FULLY IN THIS PLACE OF
WHERE I AM RIGHT NOW — ?
IT SEEMS DIFFICULT BECAUSE I WOULD RATHER
NOT BE SO "OUT OF STEP" — SO, OUT OF FOCUS

LISTEN, MOE TO THE
MANY INVITATIONS YOU
RECEIVE THESE DAYS & WEEKS

TO GROW,
TO FLOURISH

FLOURISHING IS

NOT JUST MAKING IT... BUT
ABSOLUTELY THRIVING... SO
NOURISHED THAT I AM GROWING
& LIVING AT "FULL THROTTLE"

FLOURISHING... HEALTHY, DEEPLY
GREEN, FULLY AWAKENED LIVING
IT IS TO BE SO FILLED & SO OPEN
THAT ALL THAT IS NEEDED IS ALLOWED
IN ~ NOTHING CAN IMPEDE THE
WONDERFUL WORK OF MYSTERY

WHAT IN MY LIFE HAS PROMOTED MY HUMAN
FLOURISHING?

Dialoging with another, even God, brings deep understanding to the journal keeper.

MONDAY, JULY 12

"Free-associating"

An open-ended journal frees you to better understand your self. It allows you to follow the free flow of fantasy, encouraging your imagination to run wild. In other words, it captures your visions and intuitive leaps of fancy. "Stream of consciousness" entries enable you to not only gradually unfold and subsequently recognize and accept thoughts, but, more importantly, make fascinating discoveries. The journal provides impetus for contacting your center. This is evident from the following written reflection by Jacqueline:

Sitting on a log in the Colorado mountains at eleven thousand feet, Jacqueline painted the distant mountains. The silence and beauty of nature lulls the artist into another dimension of no time and deep contemplation.

As an artist, now writing this, now taking a risk similar to the one I ascribe to, in other terms, using words rather than paints to express myself is not very familiar or comfortable, but it is another way of being creative and I am willing to take that risk, because I yearn to be more.

I can vividly recall a time in kindergarten when I touched the very hot radiator with my crayons, watching the beautiful liquid colors drip down. I was transfixed, spellbound. After that, drawing on paper with dull, dry crayons never gave me much pleasure. I believe that experience in kindergarten touched me so deeply that it influenced me to become an artist.

I remember copying pictures from the sports section of the newspaper at age nine because they were drawn with pencil—the only tool available to me. In seventh grade my art teacher encouraged me with kind words. But, as I write this, it occurs to me that I think for me it all really started when I was in kindergarten, watching the beautiful, vivid, liquid color drip down that hot radiator. It became an awe-inspiring, magical event that I vividly remember to this day. I remember that it was sunny and cold. I can still conjure the smell of the wax melting on the hot radiator. Those melting crayons triggered my curiosity and interest. They became the impetus, the spark that gave me the desire to study and eventually become a painter.

For the writer to explore the world of color and the artist to explore the world of words may open whole new vistas of creativity.

Doodling, Drawing, and Sketching

Doodles, drawings, and sketches provide added sources of insight into the varied aspects of your personality. Donna's journal, for example, was a literal portfolio of angel drawings. At first, the angel's forbidding pose was like that found on a cemetery's pedestaled statues: rigid, stony, aloof. Over the course of two years, the original pose softened; indeed, her angel descended from the pedestal, standing casually akimbo on the ground with a bemused smile on her face. For Donna, raised with a rigidly religious background, the angel revealed to her the strict and punishing inner censor she had adopted. She had continually dreamed of "fallen" angels and angels pursuing her for her misdeeds. Her journal drawings, tracing changes in the angel's posture from a forbidding to a forgiving stance, reflected her own emotional and spiritual metamorphoses.

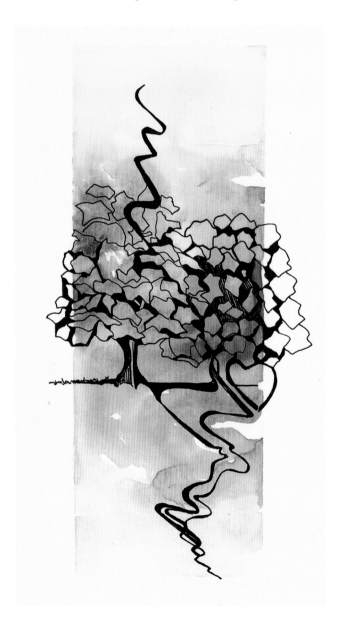

LEFT: *A symbol of love, in the form of a heart, joins the trees that complement each other to emit energy.*

OPPOSITE: *The simple, horizontal lines divide the forms, very definitely creating an "above" and "below." This right-brained, pen-and-ink doodle is rich in symbolism—flames, chains, rocks, and an ascending figure.*

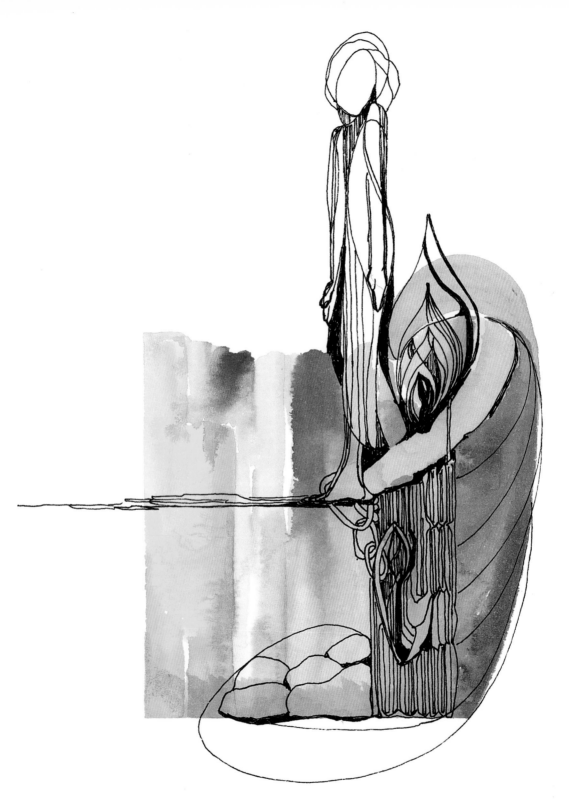

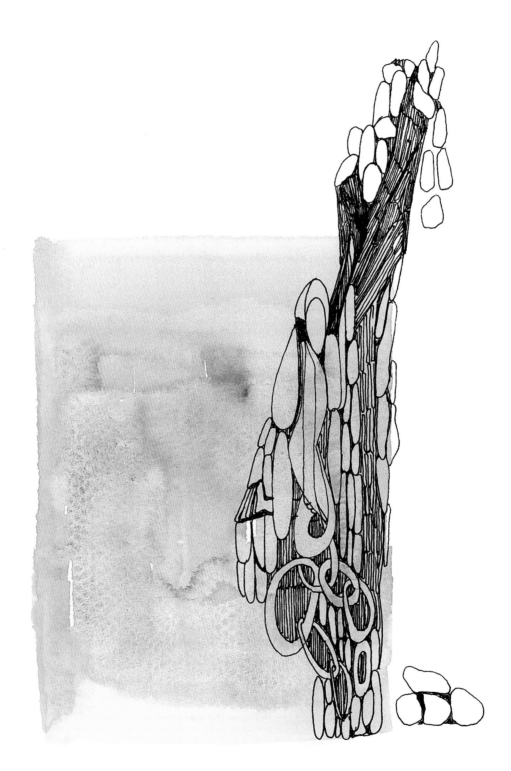

After every meditation period, begin to doodle into your journal before writing any words. This doodling seems to "extend" the quality of the period of solitude without needing to formulate meanings, concepts, and words. Notice that the usual difficulty in putting "words" to an experience of prayer or meditation is freed up because of this transition. In addition, notice that your doodles, at times, have significance in and of themselves. It is, in fact, a kind of language and, as such, can be revealing of what is happening in your life.

RIGHT: *Overlapping shapes burst from deep within this abstract landscape with an explosion of vitality.*

OPPOSITE: *Doodling helps to extend the quality of the period of solitude without needing to formulate meanings, concepts, and words. As a sort of language, it can be revealing of what is happening in your life. For example, this drawing by Maureen was executed vertically. However, one viewer suggested she look at it sideways and observed that the reclining, winged figure seemed to be chained to the earth, prevented from flying.*

SHUTTLING

When you get stuck painting, write. When you get stuck writing, paint. Shuttling between the two methods is freeing and can bring you back to the initial method more refreshed.

Sylvia, who began painting while recovering from a skiing accident that left her quadriplegic, sometimes got stuck when the brush, the colors, or the form did not seem to work for her. Raymond suggested that she try shuttling between the two sides of her brain, that is, between painting and writing. It was suggested that she write when she had trouble painting, and paint when she had trouble writing. This is one entry from her journal where she tried, successfully, to do just that.

> Today I struggle between the two—writing and painting. Painting is my first choice. But there are days when nothing happens—nothing I do makes me say, "Wow" to my own work. It is then I must shift brains and write. Writing clears my head when I am stuck with the painting. When I turn to painting I am able to settle in and allow the painting to evolve on its own. For example, my friend was moving to Florida. She was my security blanket when I lived alone. I slept secure in the house alone, for I knew Ann would come even in the middle of the night if I needed her. After she left, I tried to paint. The brush felt heavy. The paper stayed white as I stared at it. So I picked up my pen instead.

When Sylvia returned to her painting, she created the image shown at the top of the opposite page.

Later that month, when she was having difficulty writing, she painted.

Returning later to her journal, her pen then moved as smoothly as her brush had. She wrote:

> Painting provides for me a safe haven where I can regress from the world. It allows me a space to slow down and gives permission to waste time. It allows me to be—just be. It's like an old friend just waiting to play.

OPPOSITE, TOP: *Sylvia sometimes got "stuck" when the brush, the colors, or the form did not seem to work for her. Raymond suggested that she try shuttling between painting and writing. After writing in her journal, this is what happened.*

OPPOSITE, BOTTOM: *Later that month, when Sylvia was having difficulty writing, more specifically writing about her painting, she took up her brush and painted. This is what happened.*

You cannot direct the wind
You can adjust the sails

Sylvia

Trust yourself

Sylvia

CLUSTERING

Clustering is an intriguing method of open-ended writing, akin to free association and brainstorming. Beginning with a nucleus word and spilling off other words and phrases at random, complex images and emotional qualities associated with them become clear, leading to a pattern and organization of meaning not originally perceived. The goal is to cull from the cluster a self-contained statement that elucidates the original stimulus word. Clustering shapes your experience. It is an approach that forms and structures the confusion that sometimes characterizes our lives, offering clarity and direction. It helps to make sense out of random events, organize thinking, and recognize patterns. It contacts your inner processes. From it come unexpected and surprising revelations.

At our workshops, each of us actively engages in the very processes we request of participants. Following are two clusters—one by Jacqueline and one by Raymond—from two separate workshop demonstrations. These illustrate the synergistic effect of adding words to color and color to words when journaling. In the first example, Jacqueline, the artist, started with colors and then added words.

After Jacqueline demonstrated splashing color onto paper, Raymond said to her, "Put words to that." Jacqueline felt put on the spot, being asked to do something she was not familiar with—using words to describe a spontaneous creation. Nervously, as she began to draw with pen and ink on the top edge of the painting, a flash of insight flooded her mind and she wrote the following words on the bottom of her painting:

Hard and soft edges. My soft interior is protected by my hard outer edges. I see hidden pathways to enter within—grateful to be able to expose myself at last.

Almost immediately she had another spark of insight—the ink drawing around the upper edge was "camouflage." This discovery felt like a monumental happening. Her "panic attack" signified that she was at risk of being exposed. But was she? Jacqueline then wrote, "The creative artist is one who is not only skilled but someone who is willing to take the risk of being exposed—challenged."

In the next cluster, Raymond, the writer, added color to his words.

Being asked to put words to a spontaneous demonstration, Jacqueline felt uncomfortable and at risk. When she read what she had written, she felt that the spark of insight was worth the unnerving challenge.

HARD AND SOFT EDGES
MY SOFT INTERIOR IS
PROTECTED BY MY HARD
OUTER EDGES.
I SEE HIDDEN PATHWAYS
TO ENTER WITHIN —
GRATEFUL TO BE ABLE
TO EXPOSE MYSELF.
AT LAST.

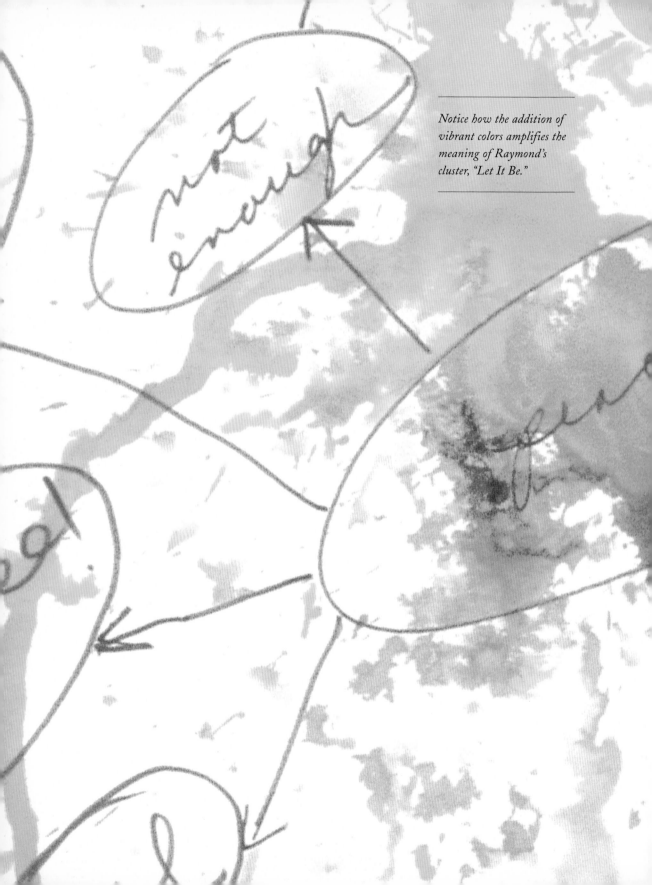

Notice how the addition of vibrant colors amplifies the meaning of Raymond's cluster, "Let It Be."

Can it be

why → distractions

beginning to happen

let it be

fright

not enough

mercifulness

not feel now

plused

too much going on

goal possible

want so much

made choices

fade away

I want to be at peace (oh! God as I write) (claim that peace) It's my goal but I wonder at times if its possible. I guess I have to make choices. Is it a priority? Please you can make it ME happen (only?). I really do I really want it. Can it? There's not enough of it. Why? I don't choose. I choose distractions instead.

Exercise: Clustering

The following is a schematic of what a typical cluster might look like. Your own clusters, of course, will be quite different from this one as well as from one another because each will reflect your unique ideas and feelings at varying moments in your life.

On a blank page, write down any word or phrase that comes into your mind. Circle this word or phrase. Remember that there is no right or wrong way to proceed—just let your mind flow. Write down any other words or phrases that you associate with this first word, each in its own circle and radiating from the first. Connect the circles with lines. Don't dwell on your choices; be receptive to what comes. If the words do not flow in any particular order, let each association find its own place. When you have exhausted this "playful" association, suspend your circling. Pull these words together to form a statement that incorporates them into a coherent whole. You'll likely be astounded at what insights will unfold.

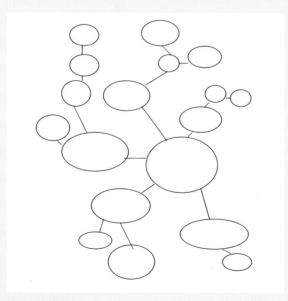

A cluster schematic

Raymond's cluster started with the word "peacefulness," the final statement reading, "I want to be at peace (Oh God! As I write this claim that piece). It's my goal, but I wonder at times if it's possible. I guess I have to make choices. Is it a priority? Please, only I can make it happen. I'm scared, do I really want it? Can it be? There's not enough of it. Why? I don't choose. I choose distractions instead. I'm not feeling it now—more distractions. Too much going on. Let it be. As I let it be it begins to happen. Let it be."

When color was dropped onto the cluster, it vibrantly came alive and the point was made for Raymond about "letting it be."

It is not a secret that there is no single route to either spiritual enlightenment or artistic creativity; there are many routes. While experiencing the journey on which your journal takes you, embrace the liberty to discover and experiment with the multiple and ingenious ways that enable you to more fully access the person and soul that is uniquely you.

Certainly, writing and words are one route, and powerful ones at that. If you choose to journal in words only, you 'll venture far. Consider, however, how some ideas suggested in this chapter, and in others throughout the book, may augment the impact of journaling with words alone, further tapping the depths of your self and spirit, and helping you to stretch your awareness and creativity beyond any expectations.

When you journal, you may be amazed at the unexpected depth and resonance that come together for you. Writing, in combination with methods suggested in this chapter as well as those of your own invention, helps you to organize thinking, clarify feelings, and recognize patterns in your day-to-day life. It enables you to contact your innermost core. From your journal arise surprising insights and spiritual revelations and perhaps the "you" you never really knew existed.

CHAPTER 4

Materials

Almost anyone can become a creative artist. . . .
What it takes is desire, determination, and
perseverance. Academic training is useful, but
not essential. Many creative artists are self-
taught, energized by the desire to create and a
willingness to take chances.

Nita Leland

IF YOU ARE a practicing artist, you'll already be familiar with the variety and range of art supplies available. For the novice, this chapter contains our recommendations of art materials to get you started. Otherwise, those who do not frequent art supply stores may be overwhelmed by the variety of watercolors, inks, papers, brushes, and other materials that are on display. You will need only a minimum of equipment to get started.

Watercolors

Watercolors can be purchased in several different forms and are made by numerous manufacturers. Some come in small tubes that can be squeezed out on a dinner plate or palette. If the paint is left out in the open, it will dry; but touching it with a damp paintbrush brings the color back to life. There are watercolor kits that have "pan" colors—pigments are in dry form in separate little pans; the color needs only to be moistened with brush and water to become liquid pigment. There are also concentrated watercolor inks that have eyedropper tops.

The amount of water in relationship to the amount of pigment determines the lightness, darkness, or intensity of the paint. More water will make the pigment less intense and less water will allow the pigment to be more colorful. The pan and tube colors are similar to one another in that they each require comparable proportions of water and pigment to create a more colorful or more diffuse mood. On the other hand, concentrated watercolor inks react to the water quite differently; more intense to begin with, watercolor inks require much more water to lighten the impact of the color. However, the biggest difference between colored inks and pigmented watercolors (including concentrated acrylic colors) is that the inks are light-sensitive and will eventually fade; pigmented colors, on the other hand, are lightfast.

The pan, tube, and dropper types of watercolor each provide the journalist with a variety of interesting effects. The choice is really up to you. (Most of the illustrations shown in this book were painted with tube watercolors or Dr. Ph. Martin's Radiant Water Color ink.)

The simple combination of watercolors, a Rapidograph pen with black ink, and tinted watercolor paper create this journal entry, entitled "Mantra." The drawing and the phrase both use repetition, one with pen strokes, the other with words, as a way of doing a mantra.

5·26·96

CONSENT TO THE HEART OF THE BELOVED WITHIN.
CONSENT TO THE HEART OF THE BELOVED
WITHIN CONSENT TO THE HEART
BELOVED WITHIN CONSENT
HEART OF THE BELOVED
CONSENT
TO
THE
HEART
OF
THE
BELOVED
WITHIN.
ASKING FOR THE GRACE TO PRAY.

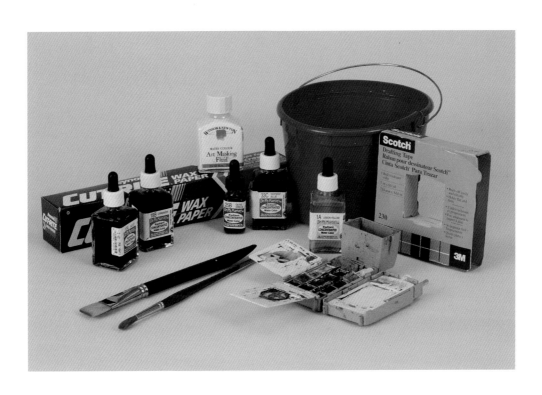

Journal Paper: Ready-made or Handmade

Paper is measured by its pound weight: the higher the weight, the thicker and more expensive the paper. Some ready-made journals may not have paper that is sturdy enough to accept watercolor or ink. If using these, be sure to check the weight of the journal paper (usually listed on the cover). Ninety-pound weight is acceptable, anything above is more desirable.

Making your own journal is the other choice. Watercolor paper can be purchased in several different weights, textures, and sizes from a multitude of manufacturers. Purchasing twenty-five-sheet packages (called a quire) of paper is more cost-effective than buying it by the sheet. An ideal paper is Arches 140-pound hot pressed paper (smooth surface) measuring 22×30 inches. The sheets can be cut into smaller sizes and spiral-bound in a horizontal or vertical format.

Brushes

There are many types, sizes, and manufacturers of brushes. To begin, you need only two: a number 6, 8, or 10 round tip, and a one-half- to one-inch square tip, both made of fairly decent imitation sable. (Imitation sable brushes are made of nylon, a soft synthetic material that in many ways performs better than the higher priced sables.) Later on, you may wish to add to your collection of brushes or try different shapes. For instance, the "rigger" and "liner" brushes have extra long tips that allow you to paint very fine strokes.

OPPOSITE, TOP: Background, left to right: *waxed paper; Dr. Ph. Martin's Radiant Concentrated Water Color; Winsor & Newton Water Color Art Masking Fluid; water container; drafting tape.* Foreground, left to right: *one-half-inch square-tip brush; number 6 round brush; Cotman Field Box (pan watercolors).*

OPPOSITE, BOTTOM: *Journals can be purchased in a variety of sizes and unusual shapes.*

Pens

A permanent, fine-line pen or Rapidograph pen, with permanent ink cartridge, is needed because it is waterproof. There are a wide variety of sizes from which to choose. For example, the Micron Pigma permanent markers come in a three-pen set with point sizes of .01, .03, and .05. Eventually, you may want to make an investment in a finer-quality pen for writing and drawing.

You will notice that both the permanent markers and the more expensive pens also come in a variety of colors including white. Experiment. Maureen uses the Rotring Radiograph pen with a mid-sized nib (point), such as .30 or .35. The range of nib sizes for this pen is from .18 (very fine point) to 2.0 (wide). The Rotring Radiograph pen uses cartridges that also come in different colors.

Permanent pens used for writing and drawing cannot be erased. Each word or mark needs to be honored. The activities in this book open paths to serendipitous opportunities for self-discovery. You cannot make mistakes. You do not need to make corrections. It is the process, not the product, that is important. Therefore no pencils or erasers are needed.

Water

You will need a container for water, and preferably two: one to clean your brushes and the other to hold fresh, clean water to apply to your paper. Transparent watercolor utilizes the brilliant white of the paper for its whites. Therefore, it is prudent to keep the water clean.

Resists

Many watercolor artists use various resist substances on sections of the watercolor paper in order to prevent the watercolor from being absorbed into an area. These resists add interest and provide additional creative alternatives for working in your journal. There are several different types of resists that you can experiment with on your paper.

Exercise: Record Your Feelings

For the more experienced artist who paints regularly, recording thoughts during and after painting can offer interesting insights. Write about what you are feeling. How do these feelings relate to your everyday life? What do hard and soft edges mean to you? How do you feel about the intensity of a color? What are your favorite colors?

Wax

If you use wax crayons or even a wax candle to draw shapes on your journal page, you will find that, when watercolor is applied, the waxed area resists the color and remains white.

Waxed Paper

This old-fashioned paper that we often use to wrap sandwiches in can also be placed over the page and drawn or written on, leaving a residue of wax that clings to the surface of the paper. When the paper is painted over, it resists the watery pigment. However, the wax in either case cannot be removed or painted on.

Masking Fluid

Several companies make masking fluid, a rubbery substance not unlike rubber cement that can be applied to paper. Winsor & Newton calls theirs "Art Masking Fluid." When the mask is dry, you can brush or splash over it either watercolor or Dr. Ph. Martin's ink.

The nice feature about masking fluid is that it can be removed by rubbing it off when the watercolor or ink is thoroughly dry, leaving the surface as it was. That area can then be painted over, should you wish to do so.

If you use a brush to apply the masking fluid, it is important to soap the brush first, then dip into the masking fluid and apply it to the area you want to keep white. The soap makes it easier to clean the brush, which should be cleaned as soon as possible.

Drafting Tape

Not only can drafting tape be used to create a border around your artwork, but it can also be altered and used to create "negative shapes." To the artist, a negative shape is an area that surrounds, touches, or separates a positive shape (such as is seen on page 34, where the artist filled in the negative spaces with a linear pattern of straight lines). Drafting tape can be cut into small pieces or torn into strips with ragged edges, and then affixed to the paper. The tape "masks" off the area to be painted and when removed leaves negative shapes.

Exercise: Dropping Color

If you wish to create a border on your journal page, place one-inch-wide drafting tape around the edges. (Drafting tape is less likely than masking tape to tear the paper when it is removed.) Brush clear water on the page, leaving some areas dry. Gently brush in or drop one color. Watch it move, radiate, and spread. Apply another color next to the first (if using a brush, be sure to clean it with water between each new color).

Let the colors run together and blend. Just observe. Now add a third color and repeat the process. Watch for as long as it takes for the colors to find their final configuration. Notice that where the pigment touches the clear water and other colors, it softly blends into them. Then notice the crisp, sharp edges where the paper is dry. Have fun, making no judgments—just observe and then write what comes to mind.

Drop, splash, or paint clear water in the taped-off area, allowing some of the paper to remain dry.

Using Dr. Ph. Martin's watercolor ink, Maureen pulls the yellow ink application out onto the page with a one-inch square-tip brush.

Maureen drops red onto the still-wet yellow area.

When a new color is added adjacent to a wet color, the new one quickly bleeds into the old one. Gently tipping the paper in any direction allows gravity to pull the colors downward. It is prudent not to overdo this process.

After several more colors are added and allowed to dry, Maureen doodles with white and black ink and writes, "Awake. . . . Listen to the silence."

CHAPTER 5

Visual Techniques

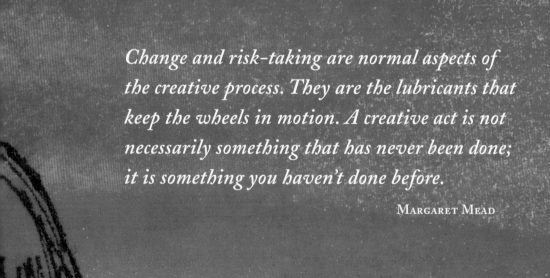

Change and risk-taking are normal aspects of the creative process. They are the lubricants that keep the wheels in motion. A creative act is not necessarily something that has never been done; it is something you haven't done before.

MARGARET MEAD

Painting techniques are nothing more than skills commensurate with printing or writing in longhand, teachable skills you learned in grammar school. Creativity is usually motivated by a yearning for something different, expanding horizons, accessing a place deep within the self. This will not be easy, and comes with considerable effort and risk.

Expose Yourself

A popular poster for a museum depicts a man in a raincoat, exposing himself to a statue. The caption reads, Expose yourself to art! Well, in a way, that's what happens when trying something with which you are not familiar, whether it be the artist using words or the writer using paints. Professional artists who want to expose themselves to different forms of art will explore different mediums and alter their styles, venturing into uncharted waters. It's disquieting and unsettling. The writing aspect involved in journal keeping may be, for the artist, a new experience that requires time, effort, and possibly some frustration. Conversely, for the writer painting and drawing may be an equally challenging new experience.

Different Strokes

As children, we were taught to use dots, circles, parts of circles, and straight and angled lines to form our numbers and letters. They were connected, broken, repeated, or made thick or thin using pencil, ink, or crayon.

Words such as *repeat, overlap, radiate, alternate, scatter, separate,* and *intersect* can give direction to your strokes. For instance, by taking a simple line or shape and being active with it (repeating it, for example), you have free range to do with it what you will. That's being creative—taking action. For the novice who has trouble getting started, using these action words may trigger creative possibilities.

OPPOSITE, TOP: *The creative use of line, shape, and form can be described with action words.*

OPPOSITE, BOTTOM: *The background is not all white or black. The closeness of the vertical lines creates a screen of gray, giving the doodle more than two values.*

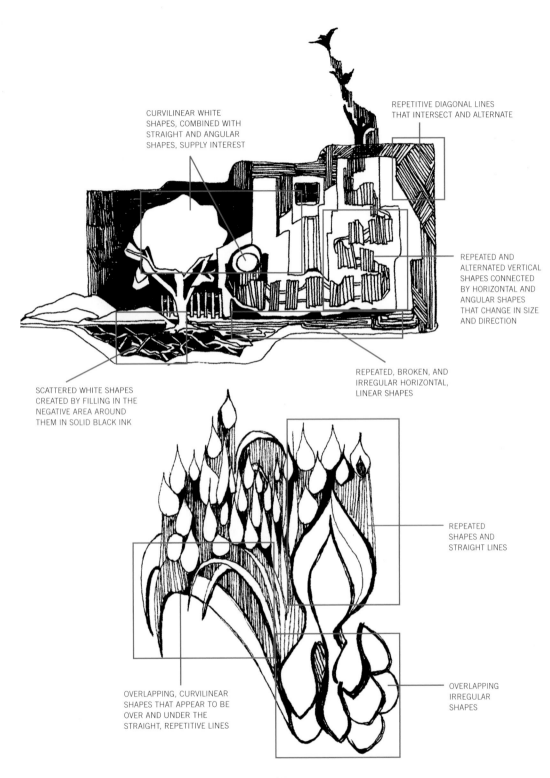

CURVILINEAR WHITE
SHAPES, COMBINED WITH
STRAIGHT AND ANGULAR
SHAPES, SUPPLY INTEREST

REPETITIVE DIAGONAL LINES
THAT INTERSECT AND ALTERNATE

REPEATED AND
ALTERNATED VERTICAL
SHAPES CONNECTED
BY HORIZONTAL AND
ANGULAR SHAPES
THAT CHANGE IN SIZE
AND DIRECTION

REPEATED, BROKEN, AND
IRREGULAR HORIZONTAL,
LINEAR SHAPES

SCATTERED WHITE SHAPES
CREATED BY FILLING IN THE
NEGATIVE AREA AROUND
THEM IN SOLID BLACK INK

REPEATED
SHAPES AND
STRAIGHT LINES

OVERLAPPING, CURVILINEAR
SHAPES THAT APPEAR TO BE
OVER AND UNDER THE
STRAIGHT, REPETITIVE LINES

OVERLAPPING
IRREGULAR
SHAPES

Exercise: Boxed Doodles

Might a little guidance and instruction activate your mind and create incentive? As we've discussed, words characterizing the many possible uses of line are: horizontal, vertical, diagonal, angled, curved, dotted, rounded, oval, elliptical, spiraled, and kidney-shaped. They can be combined, alternated, repeated, overlapped, intersected, radiated, scattered, and separated, or changed in size and direction to make patterns, designs, and shapes. And varying the space between the lines creates a gradation of values.

With a pen, fill in a page of one-inch squares with line patterns. This may be a challenge to some, a chore to others, and a gift to those of you who like to explore your inner landscape.

Do not draw. Play with lines, dots, circles, parts of circles, spirals, etc. Take one line and repeat it. In another box overlap the lines. You can radiate lines from a center or to a center. You can combine, alternate, scatter, separate, connect, and change the size, shape, and direction of your lines, dots, circles, or random shapes. Allow these descriptive words to guide your pen and trigger you into linear action. This is being creative! You will notice that time and emotion step aside, allowing you to explore "nothingness." Just like there are no two snowflakes that are exactly the same, there are endless possibilities that you can create with just a line. When the exercise is completed, quickly write about what you experienced.

You can combine, alternate, scatter, separate, connect, or change the size, shape, or direction of your lines, dots, circles, or random shapes. Allow these descriptive words to guide your pen and trigger you into linear action.

You may like to copy some of these examples to get started; from there, creatively use just lines and simple shapes.

What About Values?

Artists use the word "value" in relationship to color to define the degree of lightness and darkness. Yellow is the lightest and deep violet the darkest, while the gradations of value between white and black create different shades of gray. When drawing, the closer your lines are to each other, the darker the area will be; the farther apart, the lighter. Increasing the width of your lines from thin to thick or vice versa will have the same effect.

ABOVE: *The closer the lines are, the darker the area; the farther apart, the lighter the area. Increasing the width of the lines from thin to thick or vice versa will give the same effect.*

LEFT: *The simple curvilinear form of the tree and landscape is given density with a variety of straight repetitive lines that create value and texture.*

OPPOSITE: *These two tiny renderings illustrate how values can be achieved using only pen and ink by placing lines and squiggles closer or farther apart.*

Exercise: What Do You Mean?

It has become evident that you can describe an emotion with simple linear strokes. For instance, the words *serenity* and *peacefulness* are almost always illustrated with a long horizontal line or one that may have a very slight curve to it, a spiral, or a circle. The word *anger* is commonly illustrated with strong dark lines, exploding diagonals, or a whole area completely filled in with pencil. The word *energy,* in many cases, resembles the anger lines. What do these words and others mean to you?

Close your eyes and imagine the word *peacefulness.* How would you capture that word in linear form, without using symbols of any kind? Now try the word *anger.* And now *energy.* How would you depict *feminine, masculine, spiritual, tired, frightened, joy, elation*? What other words come to mind and how would you capture them in linear form?

Color

You don't have to be an artist to play with color. A few art materials and a little direction can get you started. As you probably learned in grade school, yellow, red, and blue are called primary colors, and orange, green, and purple are secondary colors. A combination of any two of the primaries forms a secondary. So yellow and red make orange, yellow and blue make green, and red and blue make purple.

Jacqueline measured and penciled in twenty two-inch-by-two-inch squares on a quarter sheet of 140-pound watercolor paper that was attached to a backing board. Each tiny painting, done on location, was an act of meditation; oblivious to sounds and people, Jacqueline breathed in the remarkable scenes of Tuscany and captured them on paper—imprinting them in her soul.

JACQUELINE

The three primary colors—yellow, red, and blue—are noted on the circle. Each primary is connected to a secondary color (also called a complementary color) directly opposite it on the color wheel. For instance, the opposite of red is green, and the opposite of blue is orange. When complementary colors are mixed together they become less intense, or "grayed down," as is illustrated in the center of the color wheel.

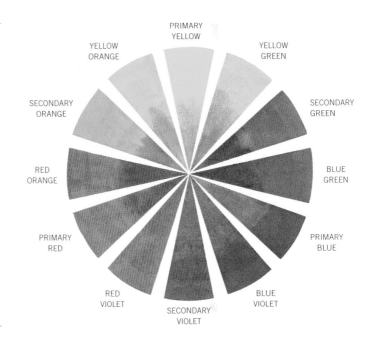

PRIMARY YELLOW

YELLOW ORANGE

YELLOW GREEN

SECONDARY ORANGE

SECONDARY GREEN

RED ORANGE

BLUE GREEN

PRIMARY RED

PRIMARY BLUE

RED VIOLET

BLUE VIOLET

SECONDARY VIOLET

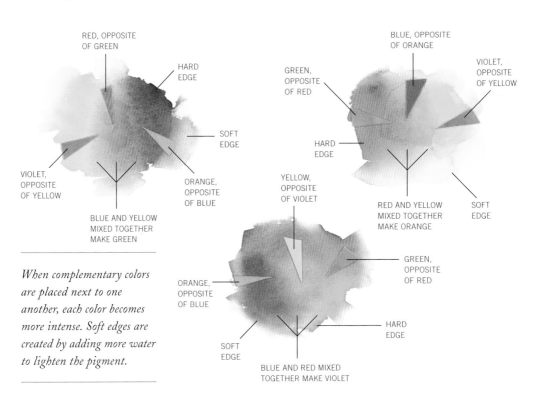

RED, OPPOSITE OF GREEN

HARD EDGE

VIOLET, OPPOSITE OF YELLOW

SOFT EDGE

BLUE AND YELLOW MIXED TOGETHER MAKE GREEN

ORANGE, OPPOSITE OF BLUE

BLUE, OPPOSITE OF ORANGE

GREEN, OPPOSITE OF RED

VIOLET, OPPOSITE OF YELLOW

HARD EDGE

YELLOW, OPPOSITE OF VIOLET

RED AND YELLOW MIXED TOGETHER MAKE ORANGE

SOFT EDGE

ORANGE, OPPOSITE OF BLUE

GREEN, OPPOSITE OF RED

SOFT EDGE

HARD EDGE

BLUE AND RED MIXED TOGETHER MAKE VIOLET

When complementary colors are placed next to one another, each color becomes more intense. Soft edges are created by adding more water to lighten the pigment.

The three primary colors used to make the color wheel opposite are Winsor Yellow, Permanent Blue, and Permanent Rose—all made by Winsor & Newton. There are twelve wedges on this particular color wheel. Notice that you can make a wide variety of colors from a simple palette of three. For instance, by combining the primary yellow and the primary blue in different proportions, you can create a green yellow, a green, and a blue green. Similarly, the primary blue when combined with the primary red will produce the mixtures found in between those two colors on the wheel. Finally, the primary red and the primary yellow combine to create various shades of orange.

Paradoxes

Life is full of paradoxes and this certainly is true with art. For instance, red and its opposite, green, are each intensified when placed next to one another. (The opposite, or complementary, color is found on the color wheel by looking directly across.) Notice how the tiny triangular areas of color become more vibrant when placed on top of their complementary colors, as is shown opposite. However, when these same colors are mixed together the result is dull and grayish. If you look to the center of the color wheel you will notice that the colors are not as vibrant because each has been mixed with its opposite.

Interest and talent are not synonymous, but many people think of them as such. Interest means curiosity, appeal, fascination, and engrossment. Talent means ability, aptitude, gift, and genius. Frequently, people who yearn to paint disclaim, "I have no talent." Is it because they really don't have the interest to develop their talent? Is it because they don't want to make the commitment after realizing their fascination requires a great deal of time and effort? You don't have to be talented to play with lines and color. All you need is interest.

Interest occurs throughout your life. For instance, a five-year old who accidentally touches crayons to a hot radiator and becomes captivated watching the beautiful, vivid, liquid color drip down, may be influenced by that one magical experience. It can become the impetus, the spark that gives the child the desire to study and eventually become a talented artist—but only after many years of study.

As Julia Cameron said, "The grace to be a beginner is always the best prayer for an artist. The beginner's humility and openness lead to exploration. Exploration leads to accomplishment. All of it begins at the beginning, with a few small and scary steps."

One Approach
to Keeping
an Artful Journal

You must give birth to your images. Fear not the strangeness you feel. The future must enter you . . . long before it happens.

RAINER MARIA RILKE

W HAT FOLLOWS is Maureen's actual approach to keeping her artful journal. You will be led into her method, including her way of doing meditation, dropping color, doodling, and writing reflections. Throughout this chapter, there are many examples from her journal to illustrate not only the art but also the various insights or movements that have occurred in her unique journey. Maureen uses a contemplative prayer method and has developed a way of incorporating the use of colors, doodles, and words in a particular sequence. It is important that you understand that this is only one way or one approach. Some may prefer to doodle first, then drop color, then write reflections, and then meditate or pray. As you read this section, you may wish to duplicate the method used by Maureen or you may wish to develop a method that works for you.

Before beginning a period of silent meditation or contemplative prayer, open your journal to the next unused page. If you want to leave a border around your

MYSTERIOUS FULLNESS

OPPOSITE: *Rich, warm colors gently brushed into a masked-off horizontal rectangle preceded a morning meditation. The result was a pen-and-ink figure, half on and half off the design, almost creating a blanket of color. A mysterious fullness?*

ABOVE: *By dropping watercolor into a taped-off rectangle that has randomly been splashed with water, the pigment flows only where the page is wet, leaving small, hard-edged areas of dry paper that form interesting "negative" shapes.*

HEART OF HOPEFUL WAITING,
  MOVING & FILLED WITH ENERGY
    TO BE,
      EXACTLY WHAT IT IS MEANT TO BE.
THE CENTER POINT ACTION OF
    THIS SINGLE LIFE OF MINE.
LOVING,
    BEYOND SELF INTO THE
    MYSTERY OF PERSONS & LIVES
  PLACED UNKNOWN INTO MY PATH.
SOME ARE SO NOT-EASY TO LOVE...
      FILLING ME WITH RESENTMENT OR ANGER
        OR
SOMETIMES SIMPLY FEELING THE NEGATIVE, AWKWARD
  ENERGY OF THEIR LIFE... EMPTY & AFRAID.
    LOVE,
      SUCH CAPACITY TO HARNESS & EXPEND THIS
BREATHTAKING ORDINARY EXPERIENCE OF
        LOVE·ING,
          BEING LOVED
      GIVING, SENDING, ABSORPING
        THIS GOD·ENERGY THAT
      SIMPLY SETS ME & US & YOU
          FREE TO BE FULL-OVERFLOWING.

artwork, either tape off a square or rectangular area with drafting tape or leave the entire page open. Then drop water into the area with a large, one-inch brush. Selecting colors from your watercolor palette, drop them into the wet area.

It is amazing to see different moods created from the combination of colors. Sometimes Maureen uses Dr. Ph. Martin's watercolor inks, which come in bottles with eyedroppers. Wetting the page and dropping in different color inks allows them to blend and move across the paper as they will. You can lift the journal and tilt the page in different directions to encourage the blending of the various colors.

As the page dries, Maureen brings her journal to the area where she prays. She takes time in quiet prayer, usually at least a half hour. Staying in the prayer position, she then begins to doodle using a Rapidograph Rotring pen (see pages 65–66). (Maureen usually works with a .30 pen for her drawing as well as

Dona, a participant on one of our retreats, taped off a diagonal shape. The color, texture, and angle seem to resemble the steep, rough terrain of her surroundings in the Canadian Rockies.

for her writing.) When you doodle, try not to be too literal with what you do, and allow the period of meditation and silence to extend into this activity. It is best when you are not "thinking" about what you are doing. Rather, let the lines and shapes simply emerge spontaneously. Using permanent ink makes erasing and changing the lines or shapes impossible; this can feel scary precisely because it is so permanent.

As stressed throughout this book, some of your worst artistic efforts can become some of your best reflections. The awareness or insight generated from them deepens self-knowledge and growth.

It is important to make sure the focus of the artwork in the journal is personal and private. It is best when done freely and not for the purpose of an artistic "critique." Surely, you may have several journal entries that are expressive artistically. If that happens, it is a bonus. The focus is not on art but on the process of self-discovery, as in the next example.

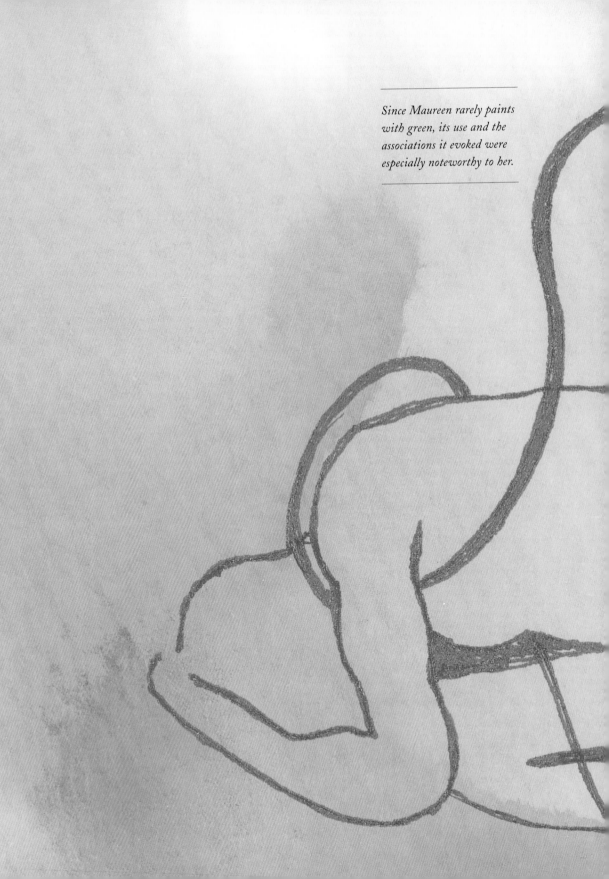

Since Maureen rarely paints with green, its use and the associations it evoked were especially noteworthy to her.

Tues 4/20

SPRING BURSTING INTO MY SENSIBILITIES,
        INTO MY PRAYER.
            IN AWE, I BOW LOW, AWARE OF THE
WAY OF MY LIFE THESE DAYS — SUCH CHANGE — SUCH RAPID
SHIFTS — SUCH A VAST & WIDE LOOK AT SO MANY CORE WAYS OF
MY LIFE... JUST AS SPRING BURSTS INTO NEWNESS,
        FRESH, GREEN — ALMOST FRAGILE BUDDING FORTH
I AM... THESE DAYS.

Once the drawing seems complete, write any reflections that may be forming. Sometimes the image is so clear that it sparks the beginning of a reflection, such as the one below.

> *Spring bursting into my sensibilities, into my prayer. In awe, I bow low, aware of the way of my life these days—such change—such rapid shifts—such a vast and wide look at so many core ways of my life . . . just as spring bursts into newness, fresh, green—almost fragile budding forth I am . . . these days.*

Since Maureen rarely uses green, when it is the dominant color, as in the image on page 89, it is especially noteworthy. Attention was paid to what associations "green" evoked. For Maureen it signified growth. Notice that the date of this entry, April 26, is at the height of the spring season. The awareness of the beauty of the early morning day in combination with the color green led to the drawing of the figure bowed in reverence. Knowing the figure represented the figure in prayer, it became evident that the growth of springtime outside correlated to the growth of springtime within.

The next journal entry evolved spontaneously as a musical "doodling," with lines forming trumpet-like shapes. Observing this, Maureen let the musical theme develop.

> *Music, lifting up and over, gliding into consciousness a melody of familiar sounds . . . as you sing my name, joyful in the formation of its melody. What is the song that is my life now?*

The process went from simple lines, to identifiable shapes, to words and meaning. This example is particularly interesting because music is an important theme for Maureen on several levels. It is a big part of her family history: Family parties have long included "song fests," in which everyone performed around the dining room table. Thus, music connotes joy and community. The musical theme also relates very strongly to the psalms that speak about music: "Sing to God a new song, sing out with violins and harp, praise God with trumpets and the sound of the horn . . . make joyful music to our God."

This musical theme came from deep within, sparking a creativity that she wanted to expand into her artwork. A series of jazz paintings evolved. One journal entry became the springboard for creativity and potential painting themes.

A musical theme sparked a creativity that expanded into Maureen's later artwork.

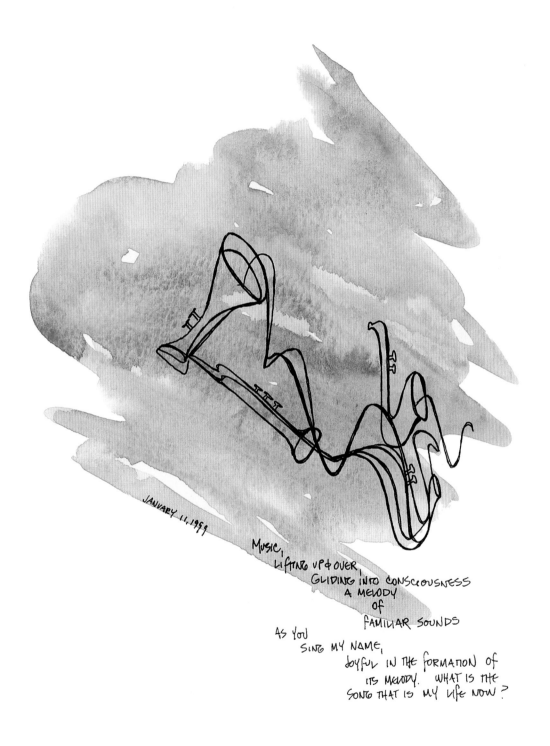

JANUARY 11, 1999

MUSIC,
LIFTING UP & OVER,
GLIDING INTO CONSCIOUSNESS
A MELODY
OF
FAMILIAR SOUNDS
AS YOU
SING MY NAME,
JOYFUL IN THE FORMATION OF
ITS MELODY. WHAT IS THE
SONG THAT IS MY LIFE NOW?

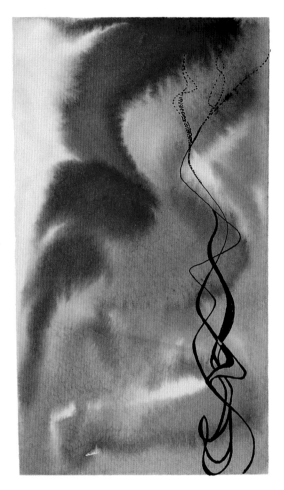

LEFT: *A combination of simple abstract lines and colors together create a mood in this journal entry. The written reflection simply extends the meaning found in the color and line.*

OPPOSITE: *Sometimes words are not necessary. There is such deep meaning below the surface as the figure above reflects upon it. To go within, to gaze into the center, to be comfortable with mystery, is, indeed, the essence of contemplation.*

WEDNESDAY 4/21/99

THESE QUIET SPRING MORNINGS, BIRDS ANNOUNCE THE DAY & THE SUN CASTS LONG, EARLY DAY SHADOWS ON THE GREENING, BUDDING LAND.

THIS SPRINGING-INTO-BEING IS HOW I AM THESE DAYS, FOCUSED, LIGHTER, "BRIGHTER-COLORED" WAY OF BEING & SO CONTENT TO BE EXACTLY AS I AM. THE PACE OF ART & FRAMES & REPRODUCTIONS HAPPILY FILLS MY DAY IN BETWEEN PAINTING. IT IS ALMOST TOO GOOD TO POSSIBLY BE WHAT I COULD DO.

YOU ARE SO IN THE MIDST OF ALL OF THIS & IT SEEMS SO RADICAL, HOW I WENT INTO A DIRECTION & WANDERED LOST & HELD TIGHT & HAVE COME OUT THE OTHERSIDE — WHICH IS SIMPLY BEAUTIFUL. THE PRIVACY OF THIS JOURNEY WILL ALWAYS MAKE ME TEMPTED TO DENY IT OR TO MINIMIZE IT. GOD, MY EARLY MORNING TIME WITH YOU IS AS SPRING...

BUDDING SOMETHING BRAND NEW — COLORS & SONG.

Sometimes, drawing is a simple formulation of several lines, while the writing is a more important part of the process that particular day. The journal entry at left shows how simple abstract lines and the combination of colors blend together to create a mood. The written reflection simply extends the meaning found in the color and line.

Wednesday, 4/21
  This quiet spring morning, birds announce the day and the sun casts long, early day shadows on the greening, budding land. This springing-into-being is how I am these days, focused, lighter, [a] "brighter-colored" way of being, and so content to be exactly as I am.

It is important to begin a reflection period with a "contemplative" stance and then write about the feeling that is expressed in the art. Perhaps only phrases or partial thoughts may emerge. Sometimes, a line from a psalm or from Scripture written down will evoke a reflection on its meaning. Sometimes reflections are more poetic in nature. Sometimes they are very literal. Again, the particular day, the particular mood, the particular way of being will dictate your type of reflection.

It is best to have a journal filled with very different, very dissimilar colors, images, and writing. It is an affirmation of the degree to which you are allowing your inner self its way in the journal. For surely, this "inner self" is infinitely more creative than you can imagine. When you allow yourself to give voice to this true self, you will be surprised by its messages, its wisdom, and its truth. Truly, all that you need to know is found within. You simply need to trust its movements and direction. Your capacity to "let go" of as much of your "daily self"— your functional, ego-driven self— as possible provides the gateway into this deeper, richer, and more authentic world of your true self.

Integrating the Journal's Journey

A sacred space is any space that is set apart from the usual context of life. . . . You really don't have a sacred space, a rescue land, until you find somewhere to be that's not a wasteland, some field of action where there is a spring of ambrosia—a joy that comes from inside, not something external that puts joy into you—a place that lets you experience your own will and your own intention.

JOSEPH CAMPBELL

ALL OF US, at one time or another, yearn for a "safehouse," a "healing place," a "sacred space," as Joseph Campbell calls it, where literally, figuratively, and spiritually we can re-create ourselves. Your journal is such a place.

When you contemplate your journal, study it; learn from it. It becomes your beacon, your compass, your anchorage. It becomes your teacher and your friend. It allows you to commune with *you*. The simple act of journaling is itself a transformational process and a distinct form of artistic expression. When reverenced it brings you full circle into becoming whole. You can enjoy freedom of expression, locate your deepest, truest feelings, celebrate your own creative voice, and discover the hidden corners of your soul.

Steps Toward Fuller Integration

T. S. Eliot recognized "we shall not cease from exploration and the end of all our exploring will be to arrive where we started and know the place for the first time"; therefore, look over your journal entries. Let your inner eye meander over the whole. It is a revelation. Do so in three distinctly different, but mutually beneficial, ways:

First, take note of color and mood. Perhaps you have been in an "earth-tone" mood. This might suggest being rooted, wanting to be grounded or contained. Perhaps your colors are pastel and subtle, suggesting tentativeness. You might be using very strong and vibrant color combinations at another point. Obviously, there is rich meaning in the interpretation of colors.

Next, read the daily entries and underline words or phrases that seem to reappear. This method of review is not so concerned with the daily contents of the journal as with the hints given about directions, feelings, or thoughts. For example, Maureen went through a period of drawings and writings containing a musical theme (see pages 90–91): Use of the word "melody" was repeated; doodles often showed lyrical or musical images. From these entries, much was gleaned about ways in which to understand the melody of her life—against the various harmonies and even in the

Take note of color and mood. Perhaps you have been in an "earth-tone" mood. This might suggest being rooted, wanting to be grounded or contained.

midst of dissonant chords. It was a metaphor that was being provided by her "inner self" to help explain current events in her life.

The third type of review is related to the content, and shouldn't be done much more often than once or twice a year. Reread your journal, preferably at one sitting, paying attention to what you were describing, how you were feeling, and what was actually going on.

CLEAR & STRONG ARE THE SOUNDS
OF A PRESENCE... IT PLAYS A MELODY
BLUES & OFF BEAT... INVITING ONE
TO LISTEN... I DO THIS MORNING...

YOUR WAY IS UNUSUAL... A MELODY THAT, AS
I LISTEN MORE, MOVES ME MORE
INTO THE CENTER, STRENGTHENING
THE INNER SELF
INTO CHOICES, HOPEFULLY THAT FLOW
FROM THIS PLACE

7.7.00

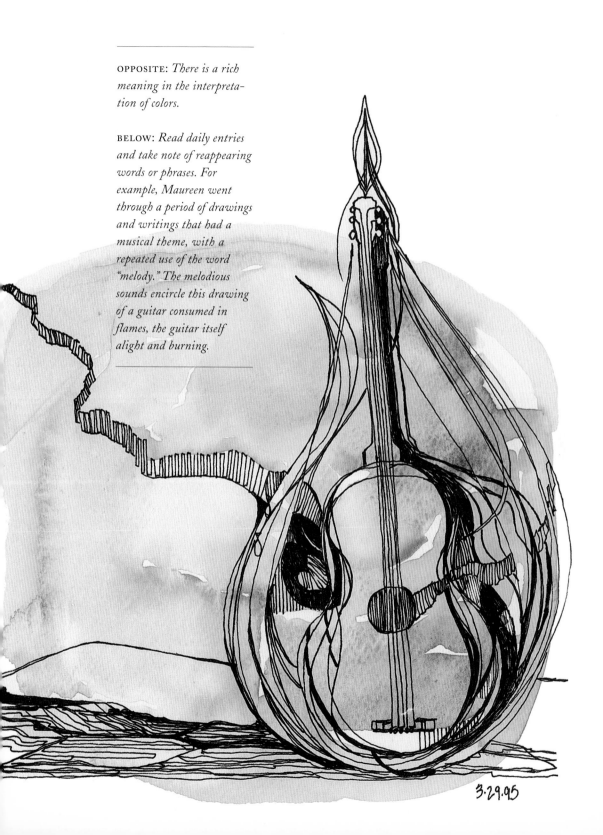

OPPOSITE: *There is a rich meaning in the interpretation of colors.*

BELOW: *Read daily entries and take note of reappearing words or phrases. For example, Maureen went through a period of drawings and writings that had a musical theme, with a repeated use of the word "melody." The melodious sounds encircle this drawing of a guitar consumed in flames, the guitar itself alight and burning.*

3·29·95

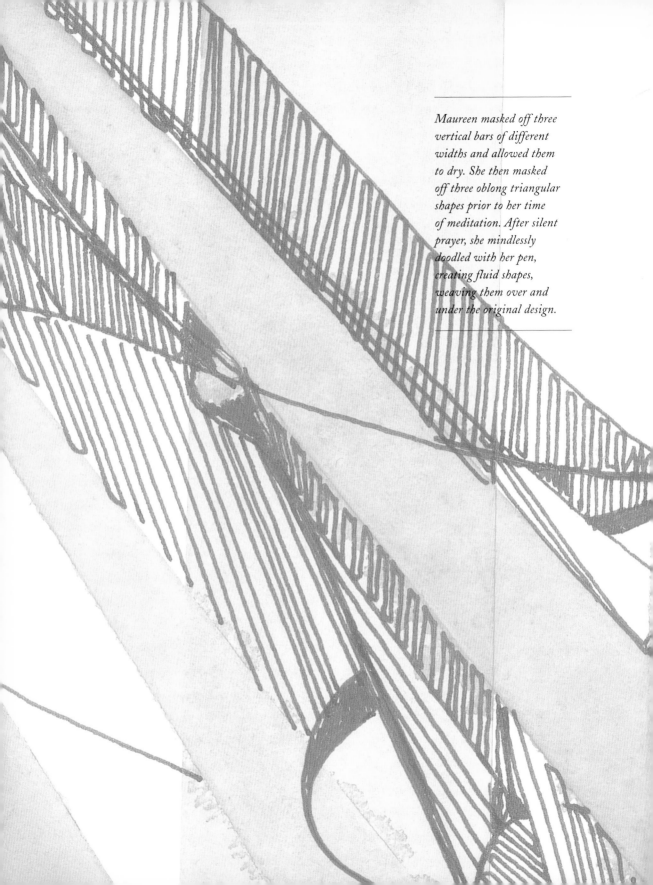

Maureen masked off three vertical bars of different widths and allowed them to dry. She then masked off three oblong triangular shapes prior to her time of meditation. After silent prayer, she mindlessly doodled with her pen, creating fluid shapes, weaving them over and under the original design.

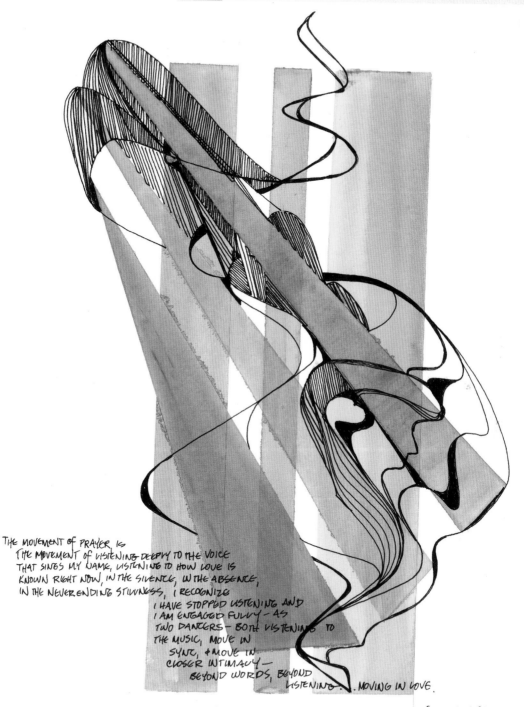

THE MOVEMENT OF PRAYER IS
THE MOVEMENT OF LISTENING DEEPLY TO THE VOICE
THAT SINGS MY NAME, LISTENING TO HOW LOVE IS
KNOWN RIGHT NOW, IN THE SILENCE, IN THE ABSENCE,
IN THE NEVERENDING STILLNESS, I RECOGNIZE
            I HAVE STOPPED LISTENING AND
            I AM ENGAGED FULLY — AS
            TWO DANCERS — BOTH LISTENING TO
            THE MUSIC, MOVE IN
                SYNC, & MOVE IN
            CLOSER INTIMACY —
                BEYOND WORDS, BEYOND
                    LISTENING . . . MOVING IN LOVE.

                            BEDFORD, 5.12.98

As you review entries over a given period, you may begin to see consistent ways in which you are reacting to a situation, or you may discover seeds of profound growth that may have been overlooked in your daily entries. Sometimes, important but small revelations are recorded that later on help you to see something much more clearly. As you journal each day, you have only the vantage point of the past along with that particular day; therefore it is extremely important to occasionally read it all from beginning to end in order to get yet a broader perspective that can only come over time.

At one workshop, Raymond shared Eliot's words cited on page 96. Requoting these words, one participant wrote: "That phrase was key for me. Because I knew, somewhere within me, that just that was likely to be my own experience. At that time, I was uncertain as to whether or not I would return to my marriage—however, within two months, I did. I continued my journal and added to Eliot's words: At the end of our exploring we will arrive where we had begun with a deeper understanding of ourselves, happiness, and contentment. . . . And so . . . let the journey continue . . . ."

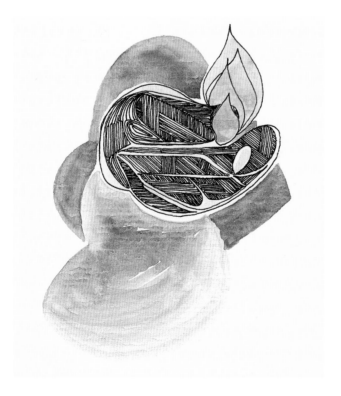

LEFT: *This intricately designed interior space suggests structure, perhaps the chambers of a throbbing heart.*

OPPOSITE: *The realistic floral drawing emphasizes looking at reality—to see things as they really are, not as others see reality.*

TO BE AWAKE,
    TO SEE, REALLY SEE — LIFE, & MY
    LIFE, AS IT IS, AS FULLY AS I CAN — IT   SEPT. 12, 1995
    WILL FREE ME TO LET IT GO SO I WON'T
    CLING TO IT. I DO NOT NEED TO BE
    DEFINED BY THE OPINIONS ~ GOOD OR POOR,
    OF OTHERS & THOSE OTHERS CAN BE THOSE THAT I
    DEEPLY ADMIRE OR THOSE I SEEK APPROVAL FROM ~
TO BE AWAKE ~ IS TO KNOW THE REAL,
        TO LIVE FULLY ONLY AS I AM

3·12·95

AWAKE IN THE PRESENCE
OF GOD

This ink drawing is an extension of Maureen's time in meditation. The figure's shape is held within a flame, aware, yet separate from the landscape.

A more permanent, personal, inner "safehouse" allows you to venture out on your own with a lasting sense of being at home with yourself. The embryonic posture of the figure on this journal page is subordinate to the powerful, colorful force that emanates from it.

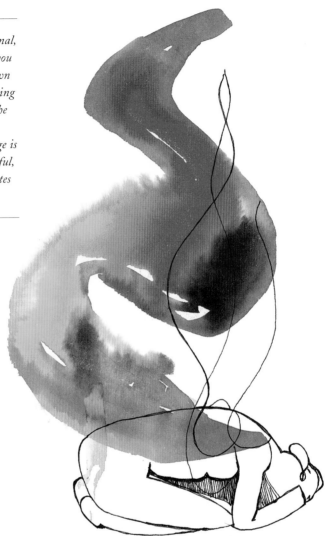

SATURDAY MORNING

LIFTING UP MY SPIRIT THIS MORNING, I AM
COMING HOME. I AM SO MUCH MORE AT PEACE
IN MY LIFE & ITS UNFOLDING.
ITS MYSTERY IS AWESOME; ITS DIRECTION
EVER DIFFERENT & KEEPS ME CONSTANTLY
LISTENING.
GOD OF MY RICHEST SPIRIT & MY DEEPEST
POVERTY - I LET GO OF MY WAY & EMBRACE THE
WAY OF THIS LIFE IN YOU.
BE IN MY MOST GENUINE
THOUGHTS & AWARENESSES & LEAD ME... HOME.

As you now know, the most important safehouse in your life cannot be found outside of you—it is inside of you. In the inner safehouse you've created for yourself through journaling, you've come to understand and move deeper into your spiritual center. Your "holding place" offers the opportunity for candidly exploring, experiencing, and accepting your feelings and affirming your strengths. You've learned to "hold" yourself.

Ultimately, you've become sufficiently whole and consolidated in this more permanent, personal, inner "safehouse." It has allowed you to venture out on your own with a lasting sense of being at home with yourself.

Your journal has become the safehouse where your inherent capacities for hope and faith and awareness have been located and celebrated.

The "safehouse" is metaphoric shorthand for being compassionate to yourself and finding meaning and lasting truths about your self and your spirit.

In the end, positive feelings and strengths are your most valuable assets. They are the pathways to finding new horizons. Change does not proceed in clear-cut, discrete steps—sometimes there are inexplicable spurts of movement. You have a remarkable capacity to regenerate mind and body, and one of the supreme elements of your uniqueness is your ability to create and exercise new options. Your journal can help you actually rewrite your life script. It is possible to make better choices in any given situation. The safe place of your journal and its full integration enables you to do just that.

This is not "the end." This is the beginning of your journal journey.

Sources

The following is a list of reputable art suppliers. Most have catalogs or on-line services, and all ship around the country.

ASW ART SUPPLY
WAREHOUSE
5325 Departure Drive
North Raleigh, NC
    27616-1835
(800) 995-6778
www.aswexpress.com

CHEAP JOE'S ART STUFF
374 Industrial Park Drive
Boone, NC 28607
(800) 227-2788
www.cheapjoes.com

DICK BLICK ART
MATERIALS
P.O. Box 1267
Galesburg, IL 61402-1267
(800) 828-4548
www.dickblick.com

KATE'S PAPERIE
561 Broadway
New York, NY 10012
(888) 941-9169
www.katespaperie.com
A specialty store for interesting papers, stationery, and journals. They have three stores in New York City; the one listed above is their main location.

NEW YORK CENTRAL
ART SUPPLY
62 Third Avenue
New York, NY 10003
(800) 950-6111
www.nycentralart.com
Known for its extensive supply of fine-art papers from all over the world.

PEARL PAINT
308 Canal Street
New York, NY 10013
(800) 221-6845
www.pearlpaint.com
The world's largest art and craft discount center.

Illustration Credits

All illustrations are by Maureen Carey except the following:

47: Jacqueline Penney
53: Sylvia Geoghegan
55: Jacqueline Penney
57: Raymond Fox
75: Jacqueline Penney
77–80: Jacqueline Penney
86: Dona Mohr

Further Reading

Beck, Charlotte Joko. *Everyday Zen: Love and Work.* New York: HarperCollins, 1989.

Budilovsky, Joan, and Eve Adamson. *The Complete Idiot's Guide to Meditation.* New York: Simon and Schuster, 1999.

D'Aquili, Eugene G. and Andrew B. Newberg. *The Mystical Mind: Probing the Biology of Religious Experience.* Minneapolis: Fortress Press, 1999.

Edwards, Betty. *Drawing on the Artist Within.* New York: Simon and Schuster, 1986.

——. *Drawing on the Right Side of the Brain.* Los Angeles: Tarcher, 1979.

Fox, Raymond. *Elements of the Helping Process: A Guide for Clinicians.* 2d ed. Binghamton, N.Y.: Haworth Press, 2001.

Habito, Ruben. *Total Liberation: Zen Spirituality and the Social Dimension.* Maryknoll, N.Y.: Orbis Books, 1989.

Hall, Thelma. *Too Deep for Words: Rediscovering Lectio Divina.* New York: Paulist Press, 1988.

Hanh, Thich Nhat. *The Miracle of Mindfulness.* Boston: Beacon Press, 1987.

Helminski, Kabir E. *Living Presence: A Sufi Way to Mindfulness and the Essential Self.* New York: Putnam, 1992.

Jäger, Willigis. *Search for the Meaning of Life: Essays and Reflections on the Mystical Experience.* Liguori, Mo.: Triumph Books, 1995.

Leland, Nita. *The Creative Artist: A Fine Artist's Guide to Expanding Your Creativity and Achieving Your Artistic Potential.* Cincinnati: North Light Books, 1990.

Lozoff, Bo. *Deep and Simple: A Spiritual Path for Modern Times.* Durham, N.C.: Human Kindness Foundation, 1999.

Main, John. *Word into Silence.* New York: Paulist Press, 1981.

Merton, Thomas. *New Seeds of Contemplation.* New York: New Directions Books, 1961.

Padovano, Anthony. *A Retreat with Thomas Merton: Becoming Who We Are.* Cincinnati: St. Anthony Messenger Press, 1995.

Penney, Jacqueline. *Discover the Joy of Acrylic Painting.* Cincinnati: North Light Books, 2001.

——. *Painting Greeting Cards in Watercolor.* Cincinnati: North Light Books, 1997.

Progoff, Ira. *At a Journal Workshop.* New York: Tarcher, 1992.

Rico, Gabrielle Lusser. *Writing the Natural Way.* Los Angeles: Tarcher, 1983.

Wilkes, Paul. *Beyond the Walls: Monastic Wisdom for Everyday Life.* New York: Doubleday, 1999.

About the Authors

MAUREEN E. CAREY, PH.D., has been leading workshops on art, creativity, and spirituality for the past ten years and has a deep interest in the way that one's spirituality is enlivened through artistic expression. She has developed a method of journal keeping using watercolor, pen-and-ink images, and words to express her inner experience of prayer. Maureen is a professor and the chairperson of the department of social work at Molloy College in Rockville Centre, New York. She was a member of the Sisters of St. Dominic, in Amityville, New York, for twenty-five years.

RAYMOND FOX, PH.D., is a writer, therapist, and professor. He teaches a variety of advanced clinical and doctoral courses at Fordham University Graduate School of Social Service in New York City. He maintains a private practice as a certified individual, marital, family, and group psychotherapist. He conducts seminars nationally and internationally, focusing on such topics as mental health, creativity, and stress management. He is the author of *Elements of the Helping Process: A Guide for Clinicians*.

JACQUELINE PENNEY is an artist, a teacher, and the author of two art instruction books: *Painting Greeting Cards in Watercolor* and *The Joy of Painting with Acrylics*. Her works are featured in public and private collections in the United States and Italy. Penney has also gained international recognition in the print market: Over eighty of her pastoral scenes have been reproduced by Aaron Ashley, Inc., a fine-art publishing company that sells her work worldwide.

Index

GROWTH ENCIRCLES MY LIFE... BLOSSOMS IN BEAUTY, A THORN SUCH CAPACITY FOR LOVE, TOUCHING THORNS THAT HURT, LEAVING ME KNOWING HOW MUCH I NEED HANDS WITH GREAT DEXTERITY...